WEALTH
WITH PURPOSE

WEALTH
WITH PURPOSE

A Common Sense Guide to Wealth,
Investing and an Inspiring Life

DAVID ANDREW

First Published 2016

National Library of Australia
Cataloguing-in-Publication entry

Creator: Andrew, David Lloyd. Behavior Gap sketches have been reproduced with permission from Carl Richards.

Title: Wealth with Purpose: A Common Sense Guide to Wealth, Investing and an Inspiring Life/David Andrew.

ISBN: 9780987095060 (paperback)

Subjects: Wealth --Management.
Investments--Psychological aspects.
Finance, Personal. Success.
Dewey Number: 332.024

Published by Sunrise Publishing Australia
22 Delhi Street
West Perth, 6005, Australia

To Robyn, Lachlan, Jeremy and Tim.

The people who have taught me life's most important lessons,

and who make every day so worthwhile.

Acknowledgements

Our wonderful clients teach us new lessons every day. This book would not have been possible without the trust they have placed in us over so many years to help them solve complex problems, and accompany them on their life's journey. They have taught us that family and relationships, not money, are the true source of happiness.

Very little is achieved in this world without friendship and collaboration. This book is the result of almost 20 years working with my business partners Michael and Chris whose capability, professionalism and wisdom has guided our business to continually strive for higher standards - they are true industry leaders.

My sincere thanks to Carl Richards whose *Behavior Gap* sketches help make complex ideas simple. Also to Jane whose coaching has been invaluable, to Lesley whose editorial skills are extraordinary and finally to my family who encouraged me to complete this seemingly endless project.

Contents

WEALTH
WITH PURPOSE

Introduction

Wealth with Purpose

"Life is the sum of all your choices."

Albert Camus

Since the 1970s, an entire industry has spawned around the management of other people's money. Today much of the focus is on the manufacture and sale of financial products and very often the fundamental needs of investors are overlooked in the haste to generate a profit. Advice, sadly, is something of an adjunct to the sale of the product, making real comprehensive advice even more difficult to find.

Much of the financial industry is having the wrong conversation with the investing public and through this book; we want to put that right. By changing the focus from *product, price and performance* to *values, goals, planning* and *outcomes*, we believe investors will not only achieve better results, but will also be more inspired and fulfilled. In the end, real success comes from having **Clarity** around what you want to achieve, gaining **Insight** so you can make smart decisions, and building **Partnerships** with the right advisers at the right times so they can help address the challenges we all face as we progress through life.

For many people, money decisions are a burden. Financial matters can be complex, full of jargon and require a level of research most people aren't equipped to deal with. Most of us just don't have time, as we focus on things like career, family and friends.

In our business we have an unshakeable belief that real and comprehensive wealth management can positively change people's lives. Having lived this belief for over 20 years, we have observed what happens when people have a framework for making smart decisions with their money: it relieves them of the burden of having to worry about their financial affairs, it delivers greater certainty about where they are going, and it gives them greater confidence.

This book is about sharing the insights gained with my business partners and our team, to help families like yours grow and protect their wealth, share it with others and build lasting legacies. Many of the concepts in this book are common sense, but the challenge for most people is in the 'doing'. We all lead busy lives and finding the time to invest in yourself and in your family's financial future often falls well down the list.

Whether you have grown your own wealth, inherited it, or are still working at growing it, the concepts in this book will help you gain real clarity around your position and what you want to achieve. It provides a step-by-step pathway to achieving the things that are most important to you.

Many people dream about being wealthy – by winning Lotto, by growing and selling a successful business, through an inheritance – and then living the life to which they have always aspired. The reality is that most people grow their wealth by patiently and diligently nurturing their resources, achieving their goals along the way.

So often we see situations where people's decisions have been ad hoc or based on events as they arise. This does work sometimes, but it can also lead to financial ruin. A far better approach is a well thought out plan that is then methodically implemented and monitored.

Imagine how different your life could be if you had a clear pathway to financial success with written goals, a clear strategy and every aspect of your financial life in control and up to date. This book will show you how to achieve this. I hope you enjoy the journey.

David Andrew
Founder and CEO
Capital Partners Private Wealth

1. The Challenges We Face

*"Life throws challenges and every challenge comes
with rainbows and lights to conquer it."*

Amit Ray

One of the biggest challenges we face today is the vast amount of financial information available to us. Every day we are bombarded with information from the press, social media and television. What's more, much of it is conflicting. Chances are, you too find it difficult to make sense of your increasingly complex financial life. When you combine this with increasing demands on your time and constantly changing rules on tax and superannuation, the big picture isn't always easy to see.

Just imagine if your long-term financial security was no longer a concern.

The problem is, we all face challenges and we're not really sure *how* to take control of our financial futures. Let's begin by looking at some of the challenges we all face, so we can plan accordingly.

Increased life expectancy – In Australia, a man born between 1881 and 1890 had a life expectancy at birth of 47.2 years. For the lucky few who made it to 65, the remaining life expectancy was 11.1 years.[1] A lot has changed since then. Infant mortality has plummeted as medical advances have been made. A far greater proportion of the population is still alive at 65 – more than ever thought possible back in 1889 when the first age pension was designed in Europe.

Over the next 50 years, medical advances will not be incremental but exponential. We're just getting started with stem cell research, our knowledge of cancer treatment improves weekly, the printing of 3D body parts is real ... things that were the stuff of science fiction are happening today.

Increased self-reliance – When Otto von Bismarck, the first German Chancellor, introduced the age pension in Germany in 1889 the life expectancy for a Prussian male was 45. His objective in introducing the benefit was that "those who are disabled from work by age and invalidity have a well-grounded claim to care from the state". His initial proposal introduced the benefit from age 70, (Bismarck was 74 at the time and still running the country), but in 1916 the German parliament brought this forward to age 65.

Back in those days very few people ever received a benefit because, with a life expectancy of 45, relatively few people made it to pension age. State-sponsored retirement was designed to be a brief sunset to life for a very small number of survivors. Today, most people reach retirement.

But while it is true that 'we are all getting older', few governments, employers or individuals have yet come to terms with the implications of a longer retirement.

So what will self-reliance mean to us? If we're healthier for longer, perhaps we will work longer than our parents did. Governments have little money to spare, so we'd better have some of our own if we're going to live our ideal lives in retirement.

Rising health care costs – The combination of longer life expectancy and improving health care means health costs are increasing at a rate greater than inflation. Who knows where this one is heading? As the cost of health care rises, private health insurance premiums will rise, along with the gaps between what we pay and the government benefits we receive. There's little doubt that individuals will be picking up a greater share of the healthcare tab in the future.

Shrinking tax base – There's another ramification of our ageing population – the tax base that funds government services is shrinking. The proportion of the population of working age, and contributing taxes is decreasing and as the baby boomers retire, this funding issue will only deepen. Ultimately something will need to give, and the mix of tax and benefits will need to change. Australia's political parties will slog it out over exactly what should happen but one clear implication is that, as individuals, we will all need to plan for our own financial security. We will need to put the financial resources we do have to work as effectively as possible.

Long-term Inflation – Inflation has been relatively benign over the past 30 years compared with the high inflation of the 1970s. Still, the average inflation rate of 3.6 per cent a year since 1983 means a basket of goods that cost $1,000 then would have required $2,928 some 30 years on. Similarly, inflation erodes our capital. A lump sum of $1 million would be needed today to have the same purchasing power as a lump sum of $350,000 three decades ago. Inflation may be stagnant now, but we should not be lulled into a false sense of security.

Helping our children – Interest rates may be low but high property prices mean housing is increasingly unaffordable in Australia, particularly for first-time buyers and those on lower incomes. For the lucky few, help from parents and grandparents will gain them a foothold in the market. For the vast majority, staying at home for longer could be the only option. It might be time for parents to reassess those plans to downsize!

Looking after our parents – With life expectancy rising, many families will need to assist their ageing parents. Competition for institutional care will rise dramatically as the boomers age and those with money will get the best care. Wealthier individuals will use their financial reserves to have aged care services come to them, rather than entering institutional care. While we reduce our lifestyle spending in our senior years, access to priority health care will come at a cost.

The inheritance generation – As the baby boomers reach the end of their lives, the next generation will become the beneficiaries of the largest transfer of wealth in history. Never before will as much money have passed between generations. This should not be taken lightly and appropriate legacy plans will need to be in place ahead of time. Some people unused to such circumstances will suddenly be the recipients of significant new wealth. This will need careful management.

The seduction of debt – Consumers today face a very different world to the one their grandparents grew up in. In the 1950s the post-Depression and post-war generations enjoyed significant growth and prosperity. While earlier generations saved in order to buy something new, greater prosperity meant it seemed possible to have everything. The consumer debt culture has grown since then and has become the norm – to the point where many people have everything that opens and shuts, but have no investment assets to show after years of hard work.

Yet the evidence suggests that all the stuff we have has little or no impact on improving our wellbeing. The immediate reward we get from buying something shiny and new is soon overshadowed by the hangover we feel when we review our financial situation.

All of these issues point in the direction of greater complexity in our lives and, as a result, an increasing need for a simple, planned approach. More than ever, a 'she'll be right' approach is likely to leave us well short of the ideal lives we picture for our families and ourselves.

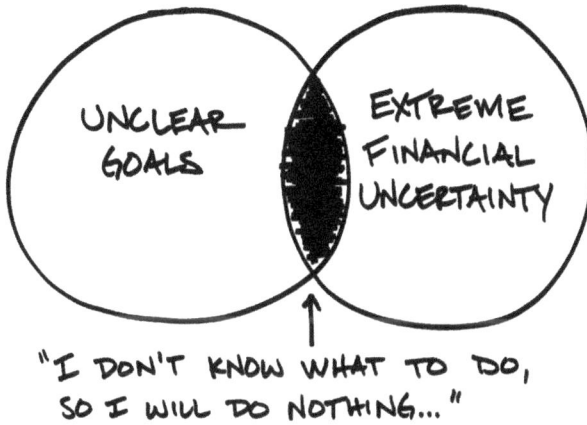

"I DON'T KNOW WHAT TO DO, SO I WILL DO NOTHING..."

2. The Solution

"Fortunate are those who take the first steps."

Paul Coelho

The term *wealth management* means different things to different people. If you asked 10 individuals to define wealth management you would likely get 10 different answers. Indeed, ask 10 financial advisers and the answers would probably be just as diverse. Most of the answers will be around the management of money and investing. While this is important, it is just one part of the puzzle.

Success leaves subtle clues, and my experience over many years suggests there are five things successful people are concerned about when it comes to money. These major concerns are:

1. To make smart decisions with their money and invest wisely. Money is too hard to come by just to allow it to be frittered away on poor planning and silly errors of judgment.

2. To enhance and optimise their position so everything they do is consistent with a better outcome. This includes their cash flow, debt management, remuneration structures, tax management and so on.

3. To protect their families and those they care about and provide the best opportunities they can through lifestyle and education. They also want to pass wealth from one generation to the next in a fair and equitable way.

4. To protect their wealth from claim and unforeseen events. This includes protecting assets from legal claim and protecting loved ones from financial hardship.

5. Perhaps most importantly, they want to make a contribution to their community by sharing their time and skills, and through charitable giving.

To frame wealth as being just about money is too narrow a definition. In this book I'm going to define wealth differently. We believe your *real wealth* is defined by the richness of your life and the lives of those you care about. Rather than measuring wealth by how much money we have, we should try measuring our relationships, lifestyle, sense of purpose, meaning and, above all, satisfaction and enjoyment of life. So while the organisation and stewardship of wealth is central to this book, it is the *purposeful* stewardship of wealth that results in the greatest satisfaction.

To deliver these outcomes we will step you through a unique wealth management model that places you and your outcomes centre stage. This is a proven model that has helped many families over many years – I can confidently say that if it is followed, it works.

Your opportunity is to implement the process for your own benefit. So let's walk through it together.

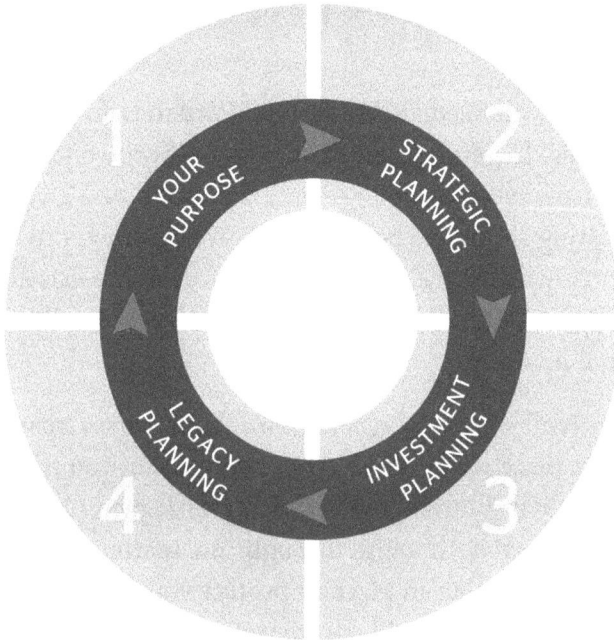

First we will start with **Purpose**, to help you establish strong foundations for your financial plan. There's no point having a plan to go somewhere if you don't really know where you are going. By completing this section you will be absolutely clear on what you want to achieve, when and why. It will also provide you with the inspiration you need to do the work required to be successful and remain disciplined and on track.

Next you will need a **Strategic Plan.** A comprehensive and flexible wealth plan is a step-by-step approach to everything you need to do to optimise your position. It is designed to help you get the most from your financial resources. Good cash flow management, tax planning and structuring can protect and help you grow your wealth. This is also the area where the right advisers can add enormous value by providing the right insights at the right times, and by helping you stay on track.

From here you will need an **Investment Plan** to help you achieve your financial goals. Legendary investor George Soros once said: "If you are having fun investing, you are probably not doing a very good job. Good investing should be boring". The investment approach outlined in this book will enable you to harness evidence-based principles and avoid speculation. It will give you an edge normally reserved for institutional investors.

Finally, you will need a **Legacy Plan**. Your legacy represents who you are, your place in the world, the contribution you make to others and how you will be remembered. Careful legacy planning ensures every contingency is thought through: no matter what happens in your life, there is a plan in place to protect you, your family and your wealth. Your legacy plan will ensure your wills and estate are in order, your personal insurance is adequate and, if it is a priority to you, your charitable giving is properly planned.

This model enables you to benefit in several ways. First it is **consultative**. Whether you appoint a family wealth adviser or not, you can engage in more meaningful conversations with your family and loved ones about the things that matter most – to you, and to them. Then your future financial decisions can be made with purpose – that is, in line with your values and key objectives.

Second, it is **comprehensive**. Rather than focusing on one narrow part of your financial life as the need arises, you can view your financial position as a whole. All the complexity is considered, rationalised and resolved in a coordinated way, with your tax, accounting, legal and investment advisers working together to ensure all areas of your financial life are in perfect order.

The last component is that it is ***flexible***. It's a wonderful feeling to know you are organised, on track, up to date and in control of every aspect of your financial life. But without occasional course corrections and adjustments you will soon be off track.

This comprehensive wealth management model is a pathway to being in control of what you have, being clear on what you need, and to having more time, confidence and freedom to enjoy the things in life that matter most to you.

3. Taking Control

"You are what you do, not what you say you will do."

Carl Jung

The answer to dealing with the challenges I have outlined is quite simple – you need to take control of your financial future. Taking control requires leadership, and this begins with you. This leadership is important to protect your financial interests, achieve your goals and to reinforce a positive money culture in your family. It also sets clear boundaries around dealing with the seductive marketing to which we are subjected.

As with just about any other area of our lives, we must accept personal accountability for managing our wealth and be responsible for the outcomes. In any field of human endeavour, leadership increases the chances of success. My strong recommendation is that every family should have a *Family CFO* (or Chief Financial Officer). This person is the primary wealth manager in the family.

As well as a CEO, every corporation has a CFO who is primarily responsible for making sure that the numbers add up, that progress and projects are monitored, and that capital is invested wisely. If it makes sense for a corporation to have this discipline, it makes sense that we adopt this thinking for our own money.

Some people will read this and think, 'there's no way I can do that – I don't have the time, the inclination or even the skill'. But everyone needs to have some organised focus on their financial success. This is where a reputable financial adviser may be useful and finding and appointing one may be an appropriate thing to do. We will discuss this later.

Whether you are your family's wealth manager or you have someone you have appointed to do the work, you will need a decision-making framework that starts with documenting your values and goals and recognises your personal strengths and weaknesses when it comes to money.

As investors, we are presented with more and more complexity every day. Economic news is continuous, good and bad, geopolitics are concerning and financial markets are volatile, so it is no surprise we are left wondering what to do next.

The answer to this problem lies in identifying what actually matters and what we can control. There is about as much point in trying to control China's economic growth rate as there is in spending your precious time worrying about things that just don't matter.

The Global Financial Crisis was fueled by excessive debt and spending and the ultimate outcome was the near collapse of the financial system. My intuition tells me that we cannot have an event as momentous as the GFC without some long-term consequences, and so we should expect uncertain financial conditions for a few years to come. With that uncertainty will come the possibility of lower investment returns.

The economy will always be uncertain, and financial markets will always be volatile and at times even a bit scary – we just need to factor this into our plans. The next 20 years will present economic and financial challenges and opportunities that only the purposeful will meet.

A clear plan for your future based on your family's values, your inspiring goals and a step-by-step action plan to get you there will be your best chance at real and lasting financial success. The remainder of this book is devoted to showing you how to achieve this.

The sooner you take control the sooner you will enjoy the results of your planning.

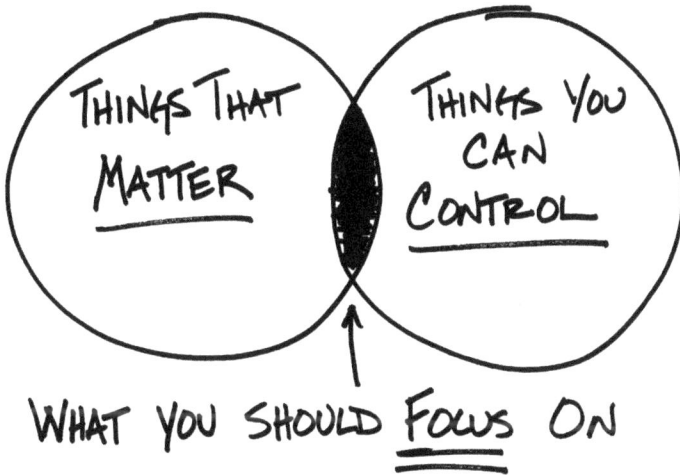

THINGS THAT MATTER ⬥ THINGS YOU CAN CONTROL

WHAT YOU SHOULD FOCUS ON

PART I

YOUR PURPOSE

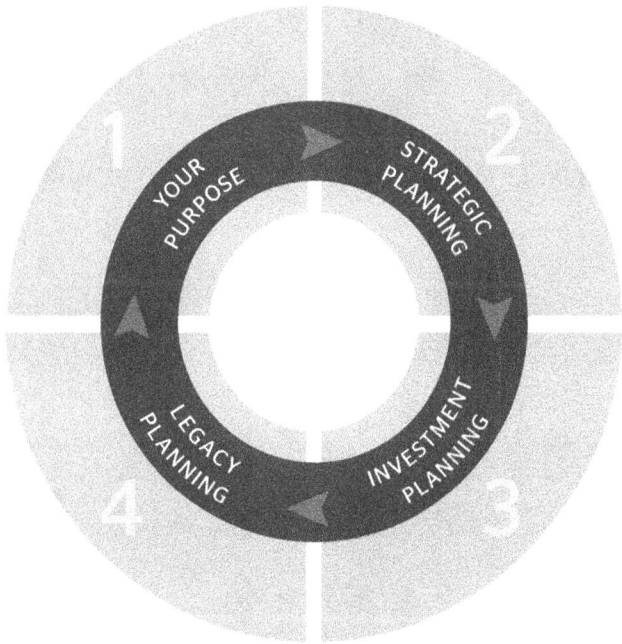

4. Clear Purpose Matters

"The purpose of life is a life of purpose."

Robert Byrne

We all strive to live our lives with meaning and a real sense of purpose and as we reflect back, the things we will value most in our lives will be our relationships and the experiences we have shared with people we care about. Understanding what drives us, *our why*, becomes the most important foundation we can put in place as we embark on securing our financial futures.

In his book *Start with Why*,[2] Simon Sinek discusses the way great corporate leaders harness the power of 'Why?' He suggests all businesses know *What* they do, many are clear on *How* they do it, but few are clear on *Why* they do what they do.

He credits Apple's phenomenal success to its clear sense of *why* – 'to challenge the status quo'. Apple's ability to innovate and think differently empowers it to be the market leader across so many consumer segments. And consumers love them for it. Similarly, consumers are rewarding Tesla Motors for its *why*, which is 'to accelerate the world's transition to sustainable energy'.

When it comes to our wealth, Sinek's golden circle is just as powerful. Most of us can clearly state *what* we are doing with our money. For example we might hear someone say, 'I run my own self-managed superannuation fund', or 'I negatively gear properties'. Some investors may even have a clear idea of *how* they manage their self-managed fund. They may say something like, "Well, I subscribe to such and such a newsletter and from that I get stock ideas, and ...'.

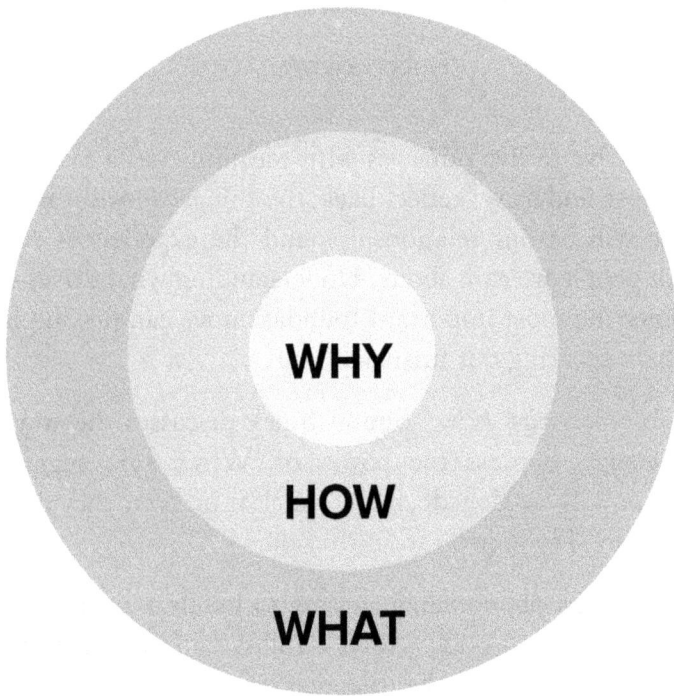

Figure 1: The golden circle

Ask an investor *why* they do what they do and they will probably respond with something like, 'Well, to get a good return on my money of course!' While this is probably true, there's likely to be a lot more to it than that.

Because investors focus too much on the *What* and the *How*, they end up making poor investment decisions. If you think smart investing is only about seeking out the best possible return on your money then you may be missing some important considerations. You may also be the perfect target for an unscrupulous rogue with a good story.

Pick up a newspaper over the New Year break and you'll see headlines like: 'Top stocks to own in the year ahead'. The likelihood of success from following such tips is almost zero, so treat these articles as good holiday entertainment but don't act on them.

Worst of all, people searching for higher returns can become victim to scams and schemes designed to enrich the scheme promoter rather than the investor. As Lewis Carroll said in *Alice in Wonderland*, "If you don't know where you are going, any road will lead you there". So let's use Sinek's idea of the Golden Circle to explain how we can make better financial decisions.

The *why* <u>always</u> comes first as it helps us define the really important things we are seeking to achieve in our lives. These may include financial security for our family, or pride and satisfaction around building a great business. Having a clear *why* should help prevent you doing dumb things with your money. It will cause you to stop and reflect on the possible outcomes before you make an impulsive decision.

A clear *why* will also keep you focused on your most important goals and give you the inspiration you need to follow through on the actions required to achieve them.

The high price of materialism

Balancing today's consumption with the need for longer-term saving is where the essence of success lies. Finding this balance is not straightforward, and to some degree society works against us.

Anthropologist Grant McCracken describes a theory of upward mobility, in which we continually 'trade up' as a conspicuous display of our rising wealth. When we buy a new home we immediately start renovating, but the new stone bench tops clash with the floor tiles so floorboards are installed, only to highlight the drabness of the sofa and curtains. This is also true when we buy personal items like clothing and jewellery. McCracken argues that the powerful marketing and advertising we are subjected to seeks to addict us to the tyranny of luxury and he warns against becoming her slave.

According to psychologist Tim Kasser,[3] if your aim in life is to be rich, have lots of stuff, be popular or good looking, then you are destined to be pretty miserable. His findings suggest that if we follow this path we incorporate the messages of consumer society into our own value and belief systems, and they then begin to organise our lives by influencing the goals we pursue. This can affect the attitudes we have towards people and objects and change our behaviours.

Kasser goes on to quote Professor Alexander Astin, who over 30 years asked more than 200,000 first-year university students from 300 different campuses: "What's important in life?" The percentage of students who believed it was important or essential to "develop a meaningful philosophy on life" dropped from over 80 per cent in the 1960s to about 40 per cent in the 1990s. Conversely, the percentage who believed it was important or essential to be "very well off financially" rose from just under 40 per cent to over 70 per cent.

Unfortunately, the road to happiness is not clearly signposted. Kasser relates three sets of fundamental needs for the wellbeing and happiness of humans:

1. *Need for safety, security and sustenance.* These are the essentials of life – food on the table, a dry place to sleep and clothing to keep warm.

2. *Need for competence, efficacy and self-esteem.* This is the feeling that we are capable, self-reliant and able to do what we set out to do and achieve the things we value.

3. *Need for connectedness, autonomy and authenticity.* We need to pursue interests and work that challenge us, and where we can express ourselves and feel a sense of control and ownership.

Need
for
connectedness,
autonomy &
authenticity

Need for competence,
efficacy & self-esteem

Need for safety, security
& sustenance

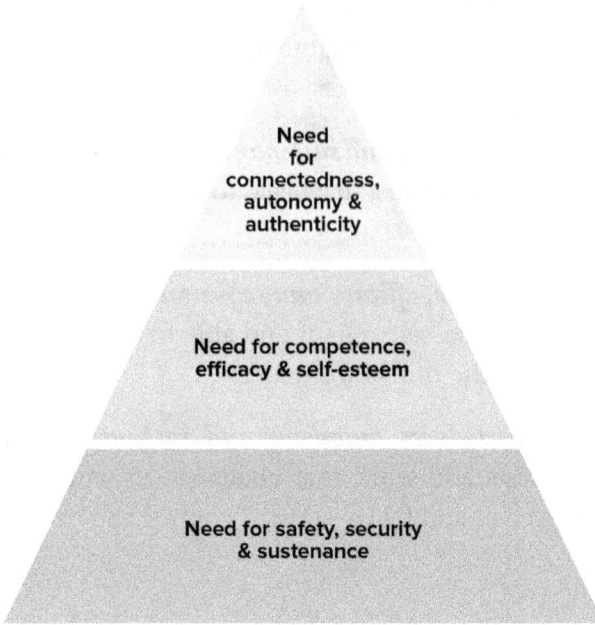

Figure 2: Kasser's fundamental needs for human wellbeing.

The relentless noise of our consumer marketing culture drowns out these basic needs and reinforces the message that our needs can only be met by buying more. Want to feel successful? Buy that new car. Want to feel good about yourself? Buy this brand of cosmetics.

This behaviour is behind the term 'keeping up with the Joneses'. Kasser concludes that when people feel the emptiness of materialism they often persist in the belief that one day, magic will happen and happiness will result.

You might think this issue only applies to those growing their wealth. It is true that the balance between spending now and saving for the future is a bigger issue for wealth accumulators than those who already have money, but those with wealth are also affected. When you have a lot of money available to you, particularly after an event like the sale of a business, the temptation can be to splurge, particularly when you have worked hard for many years and deferred some personal gratification to reinvest in your business. This is certainly the case for professionals like medical specialists, who go from relatively poor fellowship doctors to earning large incomes as specialists almost overnight.

A purposeful approach to our financial lives makes a great deal of sense. Ideally, your wealth will be grown, protected, enjoyed and shared in a balanced way – the way you planned it.

HAPPINESS

KEEPING UP WITH THOSE "JONES"

The science of happiness

So if materialism doesn't bring happiness, what does?

Professor Martin Seligman is considered a pioneer in the school of positive psychology. He believes happiness is more than obtainable and is the natural result of building up our wellbeing and satisfaction with life. His theory of happiness identifies the building blocks of wellbeing in his PERMA model. Each of these elements is essential to our wellbeing and satisfaction, and together they are the foundation upon which we can build a happy and flourishing life.

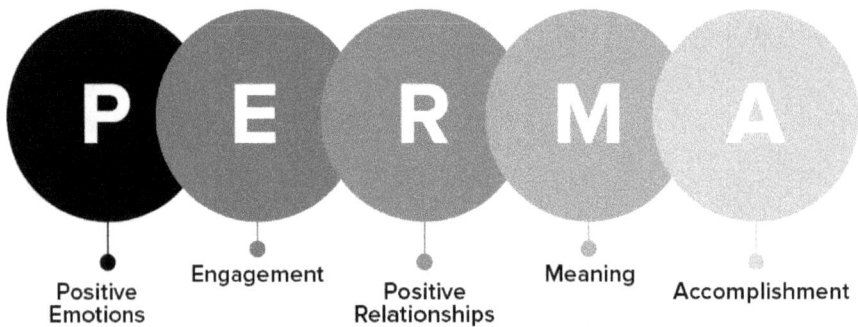

Figure 3: PERMA formula for happiness

Positive Emotions – When we are asked whether we are happy with our life or achievements, the answer will depend on our outlook and mood. If you are positive, you will view your progress to date with satisfaction, and you are more likely to look forward to the future with hope and a sense of positive expectation.

Engagement – Humans thrive when we are engaged and feeling useful. Much of the work of positive psychology involves identifying and cultivating our strengths and talents. When we identify our strengths we can consciously engage in work and activities in a way that makes us feel confident, productive and valuable.

Relationships – As social animals, humans have a need for connection, love, physical and emotional contact with others. We enhance our own wellbeing by building strong networks of relationships around us, with family, friends, colleagues, neighbours and all the other people in our lives.

Meaning – Studies have shown that when we belong to a community and pursue shared goals we are happier than people who don't. It is also very important to feel the work we do is consistent with our personal values and beliefs. Day to day, if we believe our work is worthwhile we feel a general sense of wellbeing and confidence that we are using our time and our abilities for good.

Accomplishment – Creating and working towards goals helps us anticipate and build hope for the future. Past successes make us feel more confident and optimistic about our future attempts. There is nothing bad or selfish about being proud of our accomplishments; indeed, when we feel good about ourselves we are more likely to share our skills and secrets with others.

As you begin to explore your values and goals your PERMA will provide valuable clues as to the areas of your life that bring you the most satisfaction. By focusing your energy on these areas you significantly increase the likelihood of creating an inspiring financial plan for the future and, importantly, having the motivation to see it through.

5. Your Values Drive Your Decisions

"The best things in life aren't things."

Art Buchwald

In the bigger scheme of things money is really not that important. Rather, it is an enabler that allows us to do the things that are important to us and make us happy. Values are the qualities and principles intrinsically valuable and desirable to you – in other words, life's emotional pay-offs.

Our values provide our day-to-day operating context. By basing our decisions on our values we considerably increase the likelihood that the successes we achieve will be profoundly satisfying.

Walt Disney's brother Roy once said, "When your values are clear, your decisions are easy". His premise was that having values clarity helps us make better decisions.

Money can be a touchy subject and it is rare among families and friends to have anything other than superficial conversations about it. And yet having really meaningful conversations about the role money plays in your life is an excellent starting point to good decision-making. By identifying the emotional pay-offs that really motivate you, you create the chemistry that is needed to move forward in a positive way.

For couples and families there is a real need for everyone to be on the same page. By investing time in creating this *values foundation* you give yourself the best opportunity to achieve satisfying outcomes. This is not to say a couple's values need to be identical. While there will be shared values there will also be differences, and understanding these differences ahead of time will help us understand and respect our partner when there is a difference of opinion. Failure to gain this understanding can result in conflict arising when family members' priorities drift apart.

You can establish your values by following the simple steps below.

Step 1: Identifying your core values

This exercise should be done solo, when there is time to reflect and think. Looking at the word cloud below, take time to reflect on the words – making sure you consider each word regardless of its size. As you do this, some words will resonate more strongly than others and you will begin to narrow down your preferences. Once you have narrowed down the four words that resonate most strongly, underline them.

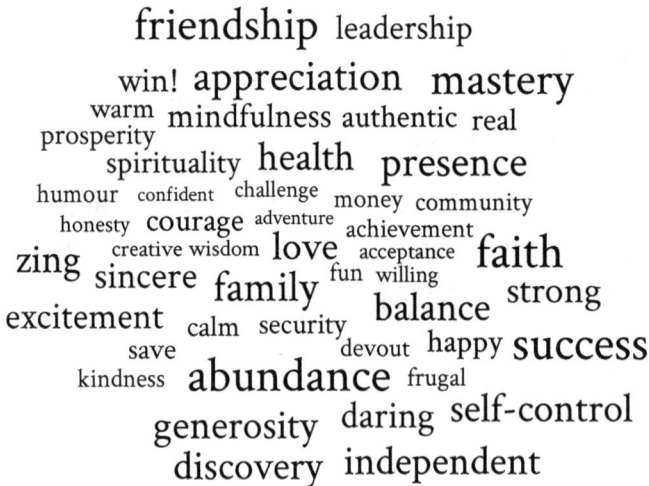

friendship leadership

win! appreciation mastery

warm mindfulness authentic real

prosperity

spirituality health presence

humour confident challenge money community

honesty courage adventure achievement

zing creative wisdom love acceptance faith

sincere family fun willing strong

excitement calm security balance

save devout happy success

kindness abundance frugal

generosity daring self-control

discovery independent

Figure 4: Values word cloud

Step 2: Identifying your emotional pay-offs

Now transfer your chosen words into the numbered boxes in the *Values Map* in Figure 5 below. Once you have done this, for each of the values you have chosen ask yourself the question: 'What's important about _____ to me?'

Let's say you have chosen *Family* as your number one value. The question will be, 'What's important about *family* to me?' Write in the empty spaces the answers that come to mind. In completing this exercise it is important to think deeply and consider what is important to you, personally.

For example, under *Family* you might write, '*Providing the best education I can for my children*'. So now ask yourself, 'What's important about *providing the best education I can for my children* to me, personally?' You might answer something like, 'So I can be the best provider I can be' or 'Enjoy the satisfaction of seeing my children do well'.

Having completed the pay-offs for the first value, continue until you have completed them all.

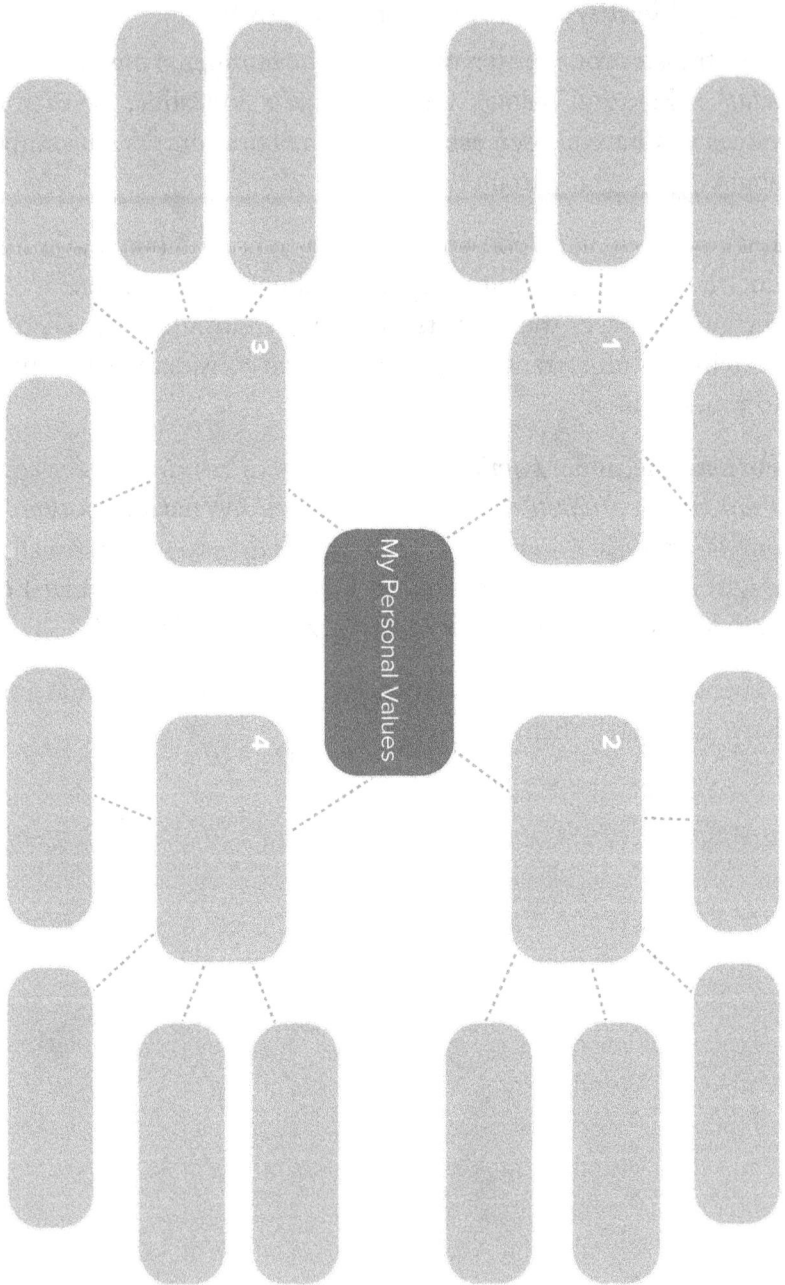

Figure 5: Values map

Step 3: Comparing notes

Once you have completed your *Values Map*, sit back and take in the results. We find that people really enjoy the opportunity to reflect and think about the things that are important to them.

If you have a partner it's now time to compare notes with them. What were the similarities and differences? How do these differences play out on a day-to-day basis as you live your lives together?

Step 4: Reflection

The final step is to reflect on the work you have done so far. As you look at the values you have documented, ask yourself the following question: 'If I lived a life in line with my values, what would my reflection be?' At this point you are likely to respond with something like, 'Absolute satisfaction' or 'I could die with a smile on my face'. It is when you have a response like this that we know you have really connected with your deepest and most important values.

The *Values Map* below provides a completed example to illustrate what you will end up with when the exercise is finished.

Live responsibly - leave a small foot print

Achieve security   Live responsibly   Have Fun!   Make a difference in my lifetime

Have freedom to choose   Authenticity   Community   Give to those less fortunate

Have my house in order   Make a contribution by volunteering

My Personal Values   Provide the best opportunities and education I can

Live an interesting life

Challenge   Family   Help my sons become good men

Try new things

Be generous

Embrace technology   Visit interesting places   Be a good husband & father

How your values keep you on track

We have had occasions in our professional practice where a client has called to request a meeting to discuss a particularly difficult decision. The decision might be about lending their adult children money, or challenges with a business partner and the like. On one such occasion a client was ushered into a meeting room, where his documented values were waiting on the table. Some time passed before my business partner was able to join him in the room to begin the meeting, and he arrived only to be informed that our client had already resolved the issue. What had occurred in that moment was that all the confusion of a major decision became easy once values clarity was applied to the problem.

Intrinsically, as humans, we know the things that will make us happy are the relationships we build, the contributions we make and the fun we have. By placing our values at the centre of our decision-making framework we are better placed to avoid distractions and instead can make the decisions that will have a more positive impact on our lives. We are also well placed to start considering possibilities and setting some inspiring goals.

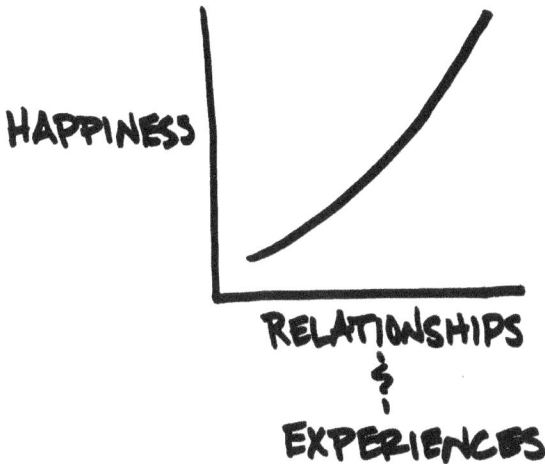

6. Creating Inspiring Goals

"Man is a goal-seeking animal. He is only satisfied if he is reaching out and striving for his goals."

Aristotle

Nelson Mandela kept a burning goal in his mind as he survived 18 years in a small, cramped cell on Robben Island in South Africa. His vow during those years of incarceration was that he "cherished the ideal of a democratic and free society in which all persons live together in harmony and with equal opportunities."[4] His goal of achieving freedom for his people was the motivation he needed to never give up, even in the face of appalling adversity.

Mandela's goal mattered – to him, to his followers and, as it turned out, to the rest of the world. While few of us will ever have a goal as big as his, we can all see how our unwavering commitment to a goal can almost guarantee its success.

Financial success is a matter of choice. For you to be inspired to take action on your goals, they need to matter to you. For you to have the discipline to pursue your goals, they need to inspire you to action within an achievable time frame. Professional athletes give us some of the best insights into the power of goal setting. To win Olympic Gold requires a disciplined plan of action and a commitment to do the work to achieve the goal.

There is no debate about who is most effective with money: those with clear goals win every time over those who drift from one decision to the next, unsure of their destination.

What if I don't need to set goals?

We often meet people who have already made their fortune and can do pretty much anything they choose. Saving money is not their issue – they've already got it. So the question goes something like this: 'Surely goal setting is for people who are still saving, why should I set goals?' This is an easy question to answer because with wealth comes responsibility. The opportunity to responsibly steward wealth is a wonderful privilege – the goals are just different.

While they may not be immediately apparent, dreams and aspirations will reveal themselves when you take the time to think through what is important to you. Some real-life examples of the aspirations our clients have pursued include the establishment of charitable foundations, helping family in a planned and deliberate way, and gifting money to passions such as the furthering of education for less privileged children.

It is also important for wealthier families to consider how wealth will pass from this generation to the next. Will it occur during your lifetime or as part of your will? Do family members have the financial education they need to take on the responsibility of receiving the wealth? These matters are dealt with in detail later, under *Legacy Planning*.

Even very wealthy people have financial goals. They are just more likely to involve spending and giving rather than saving.

Types of goals

Goals can be broadly described as tangible and intangible. In the wealth management context, tangible goals are measurable in terms of dollars and can be planned for over time. The easiest example of a tangible goal is retirement. It is easy to define, to measure and to plan for.

The example in Figure 6 is an example of a real goal. You will note that it clearly outlines what is required to achieve the goal, the time frame and the benefits. As you set your own goals, they should resonate strongly with you. In that way you will be inspired to take action, measure your progress and achieve your aims.

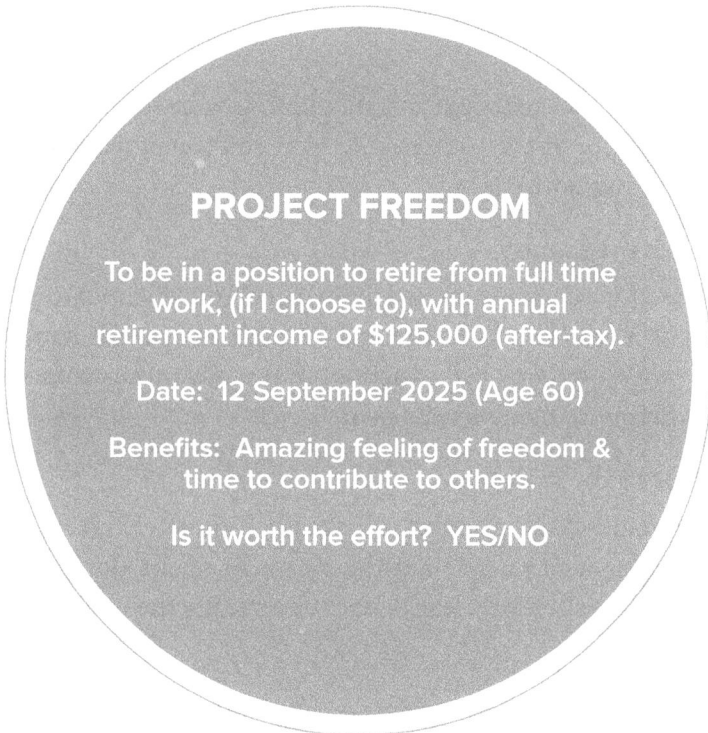

PROJECT FREEDOM

To be in a position to retire from full time work, (if I choose to), with annual retirement income of $125,000 (after-tax).

Date: 12 September 2025 (Age 60)

Benefits: Amazing feeling of freedom & time to contribute to others.

Is it worth the effort? YES/NO

Figure 6: Example of a tangible goal

Intangible goals are harder to measure, as they are difficult to quantify. An example of an intangible goal could be to *'spend more time with family'*, or *'cut out working at home on the weekend'*. Intangible goals are no less important as they often go right to the core of our quality of life. The best way to measure your progress is to document the goal and then enter into a contract with someone who can keep you accountable for doing what needs to be done to achieve the goal.

The future is coming regardless of whether you plan for it or not. Setting great goals will enable you to *have* the future you want, not the future you will get by default by drifting along.

Setting goals

There is a very clear process you should follow in setting goals. Each step is as important as others. As you set your goals, follow this process, leaving nothing out.

Step 1: Give it a name

The name of your goal is important, particularly when you are setting the goal as a couple. As in the real example above, the name of the goal becomes a rallying call to action. If it really means something to you, you are more likely to pursue it.

Step 2: Describe it clearly

Give the goal a description that makes it completely clear what you are seeking to achieve. Look at the examples of real-life client goals below and you will see a clear description brings the goal to life.

Step 3: Quantify it

There's no point having a tangible goal if it can't be quantified and measured. At this point don't worry if it is achievable or not, just put a number on it. In our retirement example above, knowing that the goal is an income of $125,000 a year after tax, gives us everything we need to calculate the capital required to fund the goal from age 60.

Step 4: Give it a date

Putting a date on each goal sets the time frame for when it will be achieved. I liken this to setting the clock ticking. From this point, each day you delay taking action reduces the probability of you achieving the desired outcome. It is best to use a meaningful date such as a birthday or an anniversary, just so you have something to look forward to once you achieve it!

Step 5: Assess the benefits

This is a test of how committed you are to taking action. Ask yourself the following question: 'Let's say I have achieved the goal – what would I be thinking and feeling having achieved it?' If the answer is something like, 'Awesome' or 'I'll feel great' or 'relief', then you know you are on the right track. If you don't have a reaction like this, you may just be going through the motions.

Step 6: Is it worth the effort?

The final step is to ask yourself whether the goal is worth the effort required to achieve it. You are really asking yourself, 'Is this juice worth the squeeze?' If the answer is 'yes', then you are ready to implement. If the answer is 'no', then you need to head back to the drawing board.

Step 7: Periodically review your progress

Periodic review of your progress will enable you to keep score and make the course corrections you need to remain on track.

At the end of the chapter you will find a number of goal worksheets for you to begin the planning process for yourself.

GOALS
&
DREAMS

RESOURCES

YOUR ONE BEST
FINANCIAL LIFE

Priorities and trade-offs

You should find it quite easy to get to your first few goals. Some goals are common to us all, such as those relating to security and financial independence, good health and good relations. Often goals just flow and before you know it you will have five or six inspiring goals ready to go.

So which goal should you begin with? This is where you may need to prioritise. But before you do, you need to understand the differences between various kinds of goals so you can prioritise the right way.

Core	Stretch	Aspirational
Retirement	Holiday home	Ferrari
Debt repayment	Private school	Motor launch
Children's education	Home renovations	
Regular holidays		
New cars		
Home maintenance		

Figure 7: Prioritising goals

Core goals are called this because they are fundamental to your security and comfort. An example would be planning for retirement. There is little point aspiring to own an expensive boat if your retirement plans will be shipwrecked in the process. Core goals are non-negotiable – we need to make them happen.

Stretch goals are the ones we'd love to achieve but there may be core goals that need to take higher priority. These goals can be strong motivators – owning a holiday home probably sounds like much more fun than 'security in retirement'. That said, most people acknowledge they probably should have a plan to achieve retirement security before they prioritise a holiday home.

Aspirational goals are the 'nice to have' goals – those you consider will enhance your quality of life if you achieve them. Cars, boats and lifestyle real estate are good examples of aspirational goals. But while a new Mercedes may be important to you, the research concludes that these items are unlikely to provide sustained happiness, particularly if the decision endangers your financial security.

Similarly, a larger home may benefit your lifestyle but there is a point at which a larger home provides only marginal increased satisfaction.

If there's not enough space for your children to do their homework in peace and quiet, then a home upgrade could become a core goal. If a new home is just about additional comfort and social status, then it would be classified as aspirational.

As you prioritise your goals, be mindful of the importance of your core goals. Keep in perspective the short-term attraction of your stretch and aspirational goals versus the long-term security your core goals will provide. We all mix up our priorities from time to time. Being aware of this and reviewing your goals in light of your values will put you in a better place to assign the right priority to the things that matter most.

Goals - the real thing

To put goal setting in context I have selected some real financial goals that we have helped clients set and achieve over the years. The purpose of sharing these goals is to provide you with some inspiration around what might be possible in your world. Not all of these goals have been achieved yet, but every single person is on track to achieving their goal within the time frame they have set themselves.

Goal	Description
'Retire with My Feet in the Sand'	To kick back and relax in retirement living close to water.
'The Big Thank you'	Two months in Italy living in a farmhouse and travelling around, spending time together enjoying the simple things. Celebrating the successful completion of secondary education for our children.
'Freedom Goal'	To be in a position from age 60 to work because I choose to, not because I need to.
'Financial Independence'	To retire comfortably at age 65 and pursue my dreams and hobbies outside work.
'Tree change'	To sell our home in the city and downsize to a property in the country, near the coast and in a community we can put roots down in.
'INSEAD'	To spend time in Fontainbleu, France attending an executive management program at INSEAD.
'Sabbatical'	To take a year off from a senior executive role to travel, learn and get re-energised.
'Helping the Kids'	Provide each of our children with a hand up, not a hand out in life, ideally to help them enter the property market.
'Portfolio Career'	By age 60, transition out of a CEO role into a portfolio career of paid and not-for-profit directorships.
'The Treehouse'	Buy a family retreat on a bush block where we can gather as a family and enjoy spending time together.
'Being Done'	By age 65 to transition our business to new owners so that we can do other things in life.
'Grandchildren's Education'	To help fund a quality education for each of our grandchildren.
'Ferrari'	To buy an old Ferrari to enjoy on weekends.

Balanced goal setting

Finding any kind of life balance in this day and age is an increasing challenge. Randi Zuckerberg, the sister of Facebook founder Mark, was quoted recently saying of senior executives: "Work, Sleep, Family, Fitness, or Friends: Pick Three."[5] She refers to this problem as the entrepreneur's dilemma, but is this seriously what the work-life challenge has been reduced to, having to choose between these things?

In our work we see the internal workings of many families, their joy of achievement and, on occasion, the raw pain of people being stretched too far. So what are we doing to ourselves?

Just because we are talking about goals in the context of wealth management doesn't mean we should ignore the other important areas of our lives. Just as a balanced diet needs all the food groups, balanced goal setting should consider all aspects of life. Each area is equally important, but at different stages of life the emphasis on one or another will change based on our current priorities.

It would be crazy for any one of us to know all the numbers we need to be financially successful and then ignore other important numbers in our lives, such as our blood pressure or cholesterol levels, or for that matter a close friend's birthday.

The *Wheel of Life* enables us to check in on our balance from time to time, by rating ourselves on each of the different areas. To complete the exercise in Figure 8, simply shade each segment of the wheel starting from the centre to indicate how well you feel you are doing. If your assessment is poor in an area you will have shaded only the first of the five segments. Alternately, if you feel strong in one particular area, you may shade all five segments. You will likely find you are completely on top of some areas while others may need attention.

This is where the metaphor of the wheel comes in, as a wheel will roll smoothly only when all of the segments are in balance. The results of this simple exercise might provide the impetus to have another look at where your time and attention is being spent so that when you consider your goals you do so in the context of a full and balanced life.

Family

Physical
Health

Financial

Social &
Friends

Spiritual

Personal

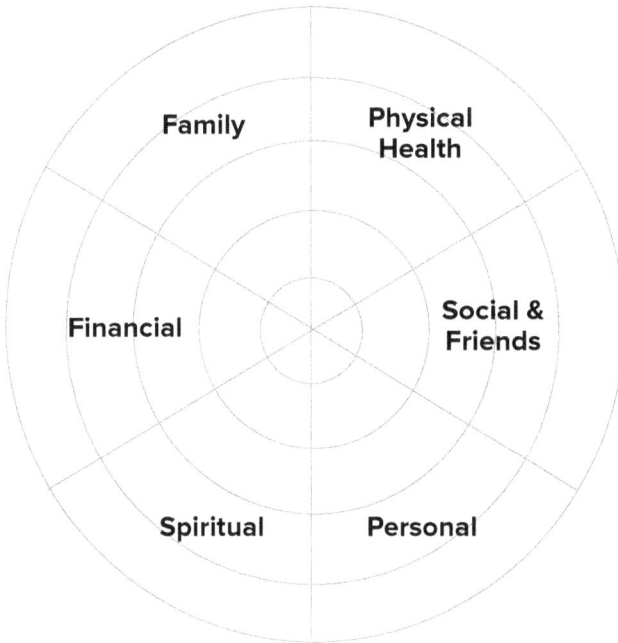

Figure 8: Wheel of Life for balanced goal setting

The power of dreaming

We all need something to look forward to and this is where a *Dream List* comes in. Some people call it a 'bucket list' and it is used to capture whatever dreams and desires come to mind. The idea is to write down everything you have ever wanted to *have*, *do* or *be*.

Dream List		
Date	**Dream List Item**	**Area of Life**
16/03/2015	Take whole family on a European holiday	Family
16/03/2015	Walk the Cinque Terra in Italy	Personal/Physical
16/03/2015	Take up weekly cycling	Physical/Mental
16/03/2015	Start an online business	Personal/ Financial
16/03/2015	Take up Yoga	Spiritual/Physical
16/03/2015	Build a holiday home on the coast	Family/Personal
19/04/2016	Lose 10 kg	Physical
19/04/2016	Retire comfortably	Personal/Family
19/04/2016	Travel the world	Spiritual/Personal
25/05/2016	Cycle end to end of New Zealand	Physical/Personal

A friend recently told me the story of an elderly lady who keeps a minimum of 34 items on her bucket list. As she crosses off one item she makes sure she adds another, so she always has plenty of things to look forward to and plan for.

As you begin this exercise don't be surprised if 'logic' holds you back. We are conditioned from a very young age not to believe we can achieve our dreams. As you add to the list, though, you will find that ideas come more easily and over time you will create a to-do list of inspiring ideas, projects and travel plans.

Writing something on your *Dream List* doesn't make it a firm goal, however. At this point it is just an idea that you may or may not pursue. The idea of the *Dream List* is to capture ideas in the moment that may later become goals.

Now we've considered *where* you want to go, in the next section we'll look at *how* to get there.

WHEN IT COMES TO INVESTING...
THE ONLY GOAL THAT MATTERS IS YOURS

Section Take-outs

....

....

....

....

....

....

....

....

....

....

Goals Worksheet

Goal name:

Goal description:

Money required to achieve goal?

Target date:

What are the benefits of achieving this goal?

Is it worth the effort?

Goals Worksheet

Goal name:

Goal description:

Money required to achieve goal?

Target date:

What are the benefits of achieving this goal?

Is it worth the effort?

Copies can be downloaded from **www.davidandrew.com.au**.

Wheel of Life exercise

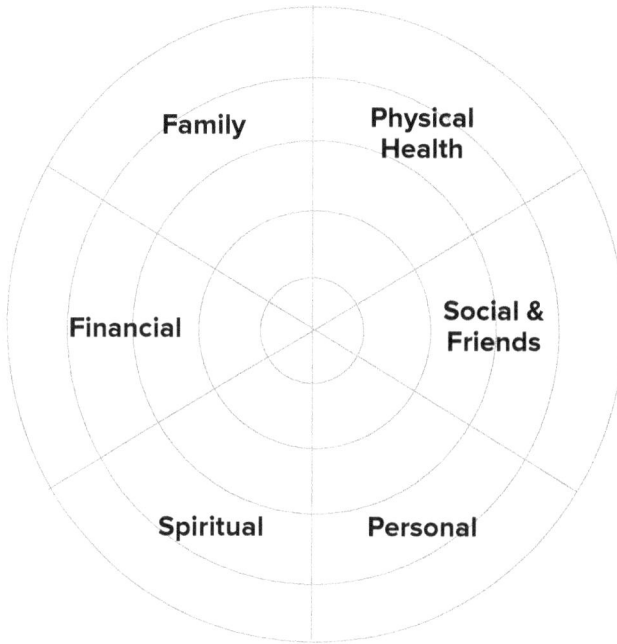

Instructions

For each area of your life, shade the segments based on how well you feel you are doing in terms of your *Ideal Life*. For example, take the segment titled 'financial'. If you feel you are doing poorly with your finances, shade one segment and if you are doing well, shade all five or any number of segments in between. Complete each area in turn and then consider how 'balanced' your wheel is.

The areas where there is imbalance, may be areas where you might consider new goals to improve your balance.

Copies can be downloaded from **www.davidandrew.com.au**.

Dream List

Dream List		
Date	**Dream List Item**	**Area of Life**

Copies can be downloaded from **www.davidandrew.com.au**.

PART II

STRATEGIC PLANNING

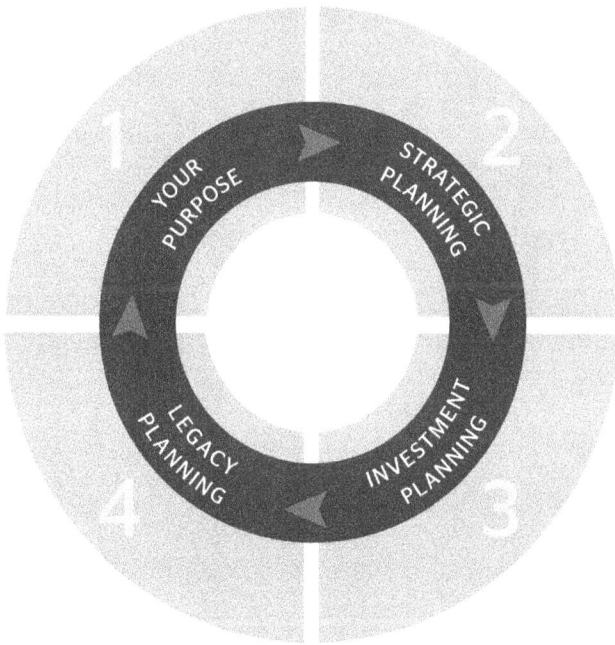

7. Creating a Strategic Plan

"Let our advance worrying become advance thinking and planning."

Winston Churchill

In business, the strategic planning process lies at the core of success. Most businesses have a strategic plan and it is the quality of the plan and the way it is implemented that guides the organisation's success. To that end, businesses invest vast amounts of time and resources in getting their planning and implementation right.

So why do so few individuals and families have a strategic plan to guide their financial success? It may just be that by the time we finish work on a Friday, we don't have the energy to begin working on our own affairs.

In my experience, few people are really well organised when it comes to their money, it seems life just gets in the way. Even those who do take an interest in money matters can usually improve on their current strategy and get a better outcome.

When a strategic wealth plan is properly constructed and implemented it should:

- Have you on track to achieve your goals in the time frame you have set;

- Maximise the cash flow available to you;

- Minimise the tax you pay;

- Have your debt properly structured and on track to being paid off in a timely manner;

- Minimise the investment risks you take along the way;

- Protect your assets;

- Provide you with peace of mind that the people you care about are provided for, and,

- Give you the feeling that things are under control.

When we are in this position we feel happier and more in control because we have greater clarity around how the future will look and more certainty that we will be OK. This is the biggest single benefit of having a plan.

Just like a business plan, a properly constructed strategic wealth plan should be comprehensive, flexible and regularly monitored. Let's look at each of these in turn.

Comprehensive

When we travel by plane we take a great deal for granted. We assume the plane is in good working order and that the maintenance crew has completed exhaustive checks to confirm every moving part and every electronic circuit is safe. Then we assume the pilot, co-pilot and engineer are fit and healthy, sober and ready to fly. Further, we assume the pilot has prepared a flight plan taking into account headwinds, fuel load, passenger and cargo weight, other aircraft and so on.

Only when every aspect of a safe flight has been considered would we expect to hear the words, 'Ladies and gentlemen, this is the Captain speaking, we have been cleared for take-off'. Can you imagine boarding a plane if you knew these checks had not taken place?

A strategic plan, too, should be plotted in such a way that it delivers the best outcome, having considered all aspects of the journey.

A strategic wealth plan covers every aspect of your financial position, including cash flow, tax, savings capacity, structures, debt, asset protection and investing to provide you with the best opportunity to achieve financial security in the time frame you have set.

Too often, people focus on investment returns with little regard to questions such as tax and structure.

In its simplest form, your plan may be an Excel spreadsheet you have prepared with a range of assumptions leading to an estimated outcome well down the track. For families with greater complexity a more comprehensive approach may be needed and can result in significant savings on tax as well as other benefits.

It is common for a well-prepared strategic wealth plan to consider a range of 'what if' scenarios and potential trade-offs between the things you would like to achieve and the things you *need* to achieve. The process of working through these trade-offs is what ends up providing you with a sense of comfort and control over the future.

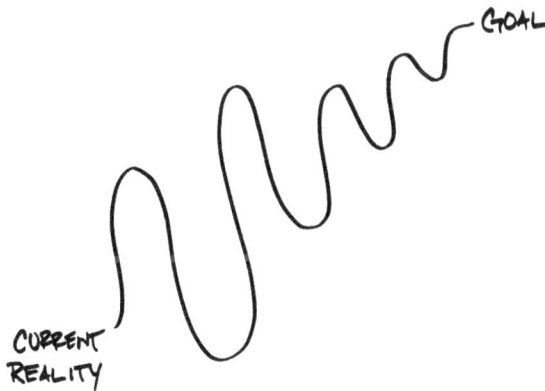

GOAL

CURRENT REALITY

Flexible

On a recent flight the pilot told me that, once airborne, a plane is off course about 98 per cent of the time. Small course corrections and adjustments by the flight crew to account for wind gusts, turbulence, fuel efficiency and other air traffic all contribute to us arriving at our destination safely and on time.

Your strategic plan should outline the best way for you and your family to reach your preferred destination with the least fuss possible, while still being flexible enough to accommodate 'course corrections' as changes come along.

Regularly monitored

It's rare that an effective strategic plan can be left entirely on 'auto pilot'. Managing all the aspects of your financial life is complex, so time and attention will be needed to get it right.

Just as movements in financial and property markets may provide impetus to check your asset values, changes in your life and personal priorities should prompt a review to ensure you remain on track. Add in changes like amendments to tax law and you will have plenty of reasons to stay on top of your strategic wealth plan.

Your relationship with money

Something you'll need to understand more deeply before you make a start on a plan is your relationship with money.

A study conducted by MLC Wealth[6] in 2015 found that Australians today define 'having a comfortable lifestyle' to mean 'having enough to do what I want when I want' – suggesting that the freedom to spend at will has become the new 'standard of living' for Australians, rather than an aspiration.

Our top lifestyle aspirations include owning the latest technology, entertainment, university education, private health insurance and eating out at least weekly.

In the study, Australian households were asked to nominate their three main goals for the future. Just under 70 per cent of respondents cited 'maintaining their standard of living' as their highest goal, 48 per cent said their mortgage was the focus, while 26 per cent nominated early retirement.

We know that previous generations of Australians did not enjoy these lifestyle elements to the same extent, so how can we afford these 'new essentials'? The reality is we are not managing this balance between living today and saving for tomorrow particularly well. The study found that 46 per cent of Australian households are living 'pay day to pay day'. Even among households with an income over $200,000, around one in five live from one pay to the next.

We also know that Australians don't expect the party to last forever, with 56 per cent of those surveyed concerned about being able to maintain their lifestyle in 10 years' time.[7]

So what is the impact of this? Our relationship with money is a key driver of our emotions, our sense of satisfaction and our peace of mind. Take this a step further and we can see how money becomes a significant driver of happiness. Let's take a closer look.

It makes sense: if your relationship with money is poor, it is likely your experience will be accompanied by a feeling of tension, that things are a bit out of control. There's likely to be overspending, regret over lost opportunities or just lack of clarity about the future. Have you ever had that sinking feeling when the credit card statement arrives and you think, 'How did we do this again?' The short-term enjoyment we get from the act of spending pales against the lingering feeling of not being on top of our finances. These feelings create a sense of anxiety, particularly if there is debt involved, and this spills over into other areas of life. Tense conversations about money aren't healthy for any relationship, so our marriages and life partnerships are affected too.

Let's flip that picture. Becoming financially organised means being on top of our spending, having clear priorities and goals, and being confident about the future. It creates a sense of calm around money that contributes to better conversations and better relationships. This leads to more fun and a sense of things being on track. It may mean there are some trade-offs around spending decisions, but in the end the sense of being on track and in control has a more positive impact than the short-term spending fix.

Once people experience the feeling of wellbeing from being organised and on track, things become clearer and decisions become easier to make.

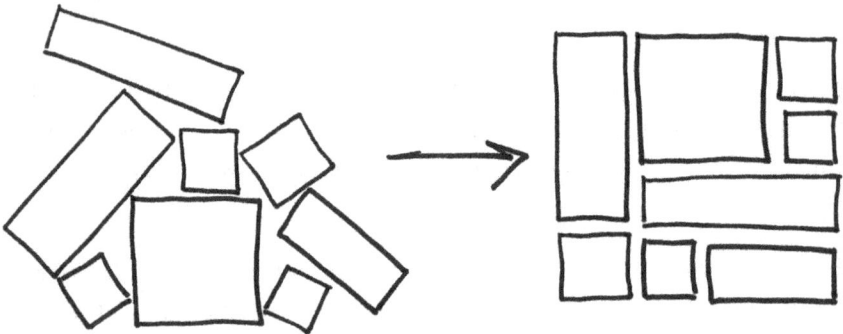

8. Making a Start

"A journey of a thousand miles begins with a single step."

Lao Tzu

So you want to embark on creating a strategic plan – what exactly needs to happen? By now you will know that the first step is to ensure you have clearly defined your purpose and documented your values, goals and priorities. Once that's done it's time to gather in one place all the information you need to start making financial decisions.

At this point, consider whether you want to do this work yourself or would prefer to work with a financial professional. (The chapter *Working with a Financial Professional* will assist if you are unsure.)

Either way, you will need the same information at hand to ensure everything is taken into account in the development of your plan. Taking a thorough approach from the start means the decisions you make are far more likely to be properly considered and co-ordinated.

The best way to establish your current position is to prepare a *Net Worth Statement*. This captures your full financial position, starting with your personal and business assets and liabilities. A sample net worth statement can be found at the end of this section.

Here is a short checklist of the things you will need to get the job done properly:

a. Documented values and goals

b. A list of all assets with original and current values, organised by ownership:
   i. Assets owned personally
   ii. Assets owned jointly
   iii. Assets owned in trusts
   iv. Assets owned in companies
   v. Assets owned in superannuation

c. Detailed expenditure analysis

d. Up-to-date tax returns

e. Loan statements

f. Superannuation statements

g. Superannuation contributions

h. Investment portfolio statements

i. List of bank accounts, noting purpose of each account

j. Wills

k. Powers of Attorney and Powers of Guardianship

l. Trust deeds for family trusts

m. Trust deeds for self-managed superannuation

n. Life and disablement insurance schedules

o. Income protection insurance schedules

p. Health insurance schedule

q. Business financial statements

In compiling all of this information you will begin to get a feel for just how well positioned and organised you can be. Knowing where things are and creating a clear picture of your position is the first step in improving your position.

Now that you have gathered the information you can review any strengths and weaknesses. The *House in Order* questionnaire that follows will help you assess the overall state of your planning and will provide insight into hotspots that may require your attention. As you complete the questionnaire you may find some areas just aren't relevant to you. An example might be that if you are 60 years of age and in a strong financial position, you probably have no need for life insurance (in which case you should score that question with a '3').

Once complete, add up your score and use a highlighter pen to mark the areas that may be of particular concern. Depending on your results, you may only require a tune-up – or you may need a financial overhaul. A score of less than 50 means you really do have some work to do. It doesn't mean your circumstances are dire but it probably does indicate you haven't invested much time in understanding your financial affairs. Things may be dire or they may not – either way it's better to know.

A score of 50 to 100 indicates you have made a good start but there may still be an opportunity to be more organised and more effective with your money. Depending on how the points are scored, you may be well on track financially but with some areas requiring more attention to get them properly organised.

If your score is over 100 you are well organised and focused on the right things. You should be well on the way to financial success.

House in Order Questionnaire

	Disagree		Unsure (n/a)		Agree
My affairs are as organised as they can possibly be	1	2	3	4	5
My values are documented and they guide my financial decisions	1	2	3	4	5
I have documented goals with realistic timeframes for achievement	1	2	3	4	5
I know exactly how much is needed to fund my goals now and in the future	1	2	3	4	5
I keep regular track of my progress and I am on course to meet my goals	1	2	3	4	5
I have control over my cash flow and I live within my means	1	2	3	4	5
I have funds available if an emergency arises	1	2	3	4	5
I have a documented plan to repay borrowings in a timely manner	1	2	3	4	5
I have the best deal available on my borrowings	1	2	3	4	5
I have my borrowings structured as effectively as possible	1	2	3	4	5
I maximise all tax benefits available to me	1	2	3	4	5
My tax is up to date and returns are submitted on time	1	2	3	4	5
My asset ownership is structured to provide an optimal tax and protection outcome	1	2	3	4	5

	Disagree		Unsure (n/a)		Agree
I have structured my affairs to protect against litigation	1	2	3	4	5
I have a clearly defined investment plan designed to grow and preserve my wealth	1	2	3	4	5
I invest rather than speculate	1	2	3	4	5
My investment strategy is well diversified to minimise risk	1	2	3	4	5
My portfolio rewards me for the risks I am taking	1	2	3	4	5
I have an up-to-date Will and estate plan	1	2	3	4	5
My enduring powers of attorney and guardianship are up-to-date	1	2	3	4	5
My family is protected with the right level of life and disablement cover	1	2	3	4	5
My income is adequately protected against illness and injury	1	2	3	4	5
I have protection for a severe health event	1	2	3	4	5
I have private hospital and ancillary insurance cover	1	2	3	4	5
My property assets are adequately insured	1	2	3	4	5
Total Score:					

Copies are available at **www.davidandrew.com.au.**

9. Planning Considerations

"Never tell people how to do things. Tell them what to do and they will surprise you with their ingenuity."

George S Patton

In all the years I have been advising clients the biggest indicator of financial success has been a family's ability to live within their means. Sometimes people make a fortune on a particular stock or the sale of their business, but most wealth is accumulated methodically. In my experience, lack of planning and overspending are the most common causes of financial plans being derailed. As advisers to successful individuals and families for many years, we have learned there can be a big difference between being wealthy and actually having money.

Many professional people – CEOs, lawyers and medical specialists among them – earn very large incomes and yet have relatively little to show for their efforts. These people appear affluent to the outside world because their lifestyles give that impression, but by any measure of long-term security and success their results are questionable. Having had many conversations with people who find themselves in this position, the answer is cash flow – how you manage yours will have a significant bearing on your future success.

Cash flow and human capital

The major asset of professionals and senior executives is their *Human Capital.* Human capital is your ability to earn and save over time. Your human capital is at its greatest early in your career. As you become more educated and experienced you expand your base of human capital. Because our productive working lives are finite, we gradually draw down on our human capital over time.

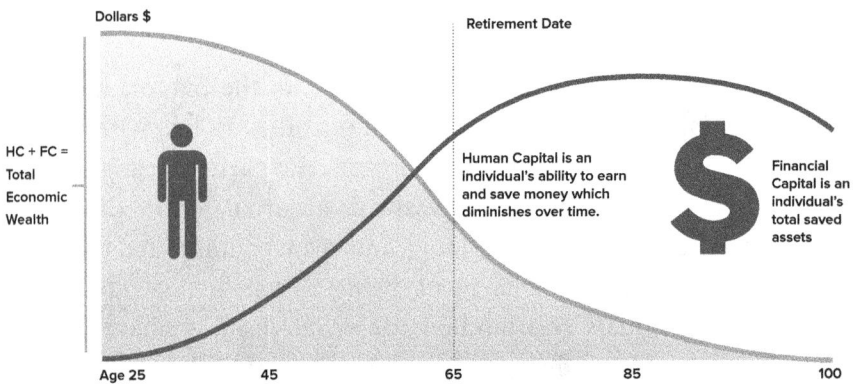

Dollars $

Retirement Date

HC + FC =
Total
Economic
Wealth

Human Capital is an individual's ability to earn and save money which diminishes over time.

Financial Capital is an individual's total saved assets

Age 25   45   65   85   100

Figure 9: Human capital and financial capital

At any point in time an individual's total wealth is the sum of their human capital and their financial capital. As human capital is spent down, there needs to be a corresponding accumulation of *Financial Capital.* Financial capital is simply your total saved assets.

The big challenge for many is that lifestyles often adjust as income increases. Bigger homes and mortgages, expectations of travel, private school education, better cars, even fine wine, are all things that can get in the way of long-term savings.

Fortunately, this is a relatively easy problem to overcome. It just requires good planning and the discipline to stick to a plan.

Human Capital $+$ Financial Capital $=$ Total Economic Wealth

Figure 10: The human capital equation

Business owners

The situation for business owners is different. Early on, many business owners need to reinvest much of their profit back into the business to fund new equipment, stock and growth. It is common in these early times to live quite frugally, as the business establishes and grows. Only when a business is enjoying real success do the owners begin to enjoy the rewards for the risks they have taken. Even then it is common for business owners to continue being careful with their money.

Depending on the type of business and the number of owners, the human capital model above may still apply. There may be a need to save along the way to achieve long-term financial security. Alternatively, a business sale may be needed to create the liquidity needed later in life. If this is the case a well-planned exit may provide access to tax concessions on the sale of a small business.

Either way, an understanding of the nature of your cash flow, and how much of it needs to be put aside to fund your longer-term goals, is an important step in creating a sound strategic wealth plan.

Understanding your spending and having a plan

Taking a closer look at habits, we know that most people just spend and then at the end of the month look at their statements to see how they have gone. If they have overspent that month there is nothing left to invest. String many months like this together and it is easy to see how people don't make the progress they should.

The first step towards taking control of your planning is to complete a spending analysis to establish where your money is going. For some people this is an easy exercise as they are already quite aware and can access their financial records. For others the exercise is mildly confronting. Once the spending analysis is complete it will be clearer whether any lifestyle and spending trade-offs are necessary to make your goals achievable.

Having gained an understanding of your habits, you now need a spending plan. This establishes how much money needs to be allocated to achieve short-term and long-term goals and therefore how much can be set aside for lifestyle.

Let's say an agreed amount has been allocated for all lifestyle expenses each month. If you allocate that sum to a bank account for everyday living it will be much easier to gain a daily picture of whether you are living within your means and according to the spending plan. This continual feedback loop creates awareness and empowers your decision-making.

Easy Money

I remember as a kid regularly overhearing the conversation between Mum and Dad as to who was going to withdraw cash from the bank teller before the bank closed at four o'clock on Friday afternoon.

On occasion we'd get caught short and on Saturday morning I would accompany Dad as he cashed a cheque with one of his friends who was the local pharmacist. The banking system meant that people really had to think ahead and plan their spending in ways we wouldn't even consider today, and as a result people were more in control of their finances and budgets. The adage 'you can't spend it if you don't have it' was the norm, particularly for those families with Depression-era memories.

From the mid-1970s all this changed. The introduction of Bankcard in 1974 was quickly followed in 1977 by the first ATM. Automatic teller machines meant we were never short of cash, and credit cards meant that for the first time we could have whatever we needed or wanted, whenever we felt like it. Whether we actually had the money or not became the least of our concerns – there was always a credit card company willing to issue a new card.

Access to money and retail marketing are so compelling that consuming has never been easier. One of the consequences is that it is easy for spending to get out of control. This just means that to enjoy financial success we need to define our spending rather than have our spending define us.

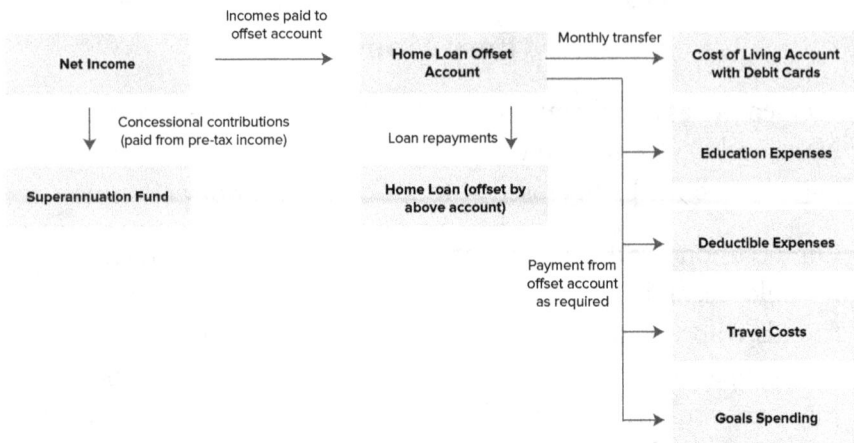

Figure 11: Spending plan

In Figure 11 we see an example of a *Spending Plan*. There may be a non-deductible mortgage, investment debt, tax payments and other commitments. In this example all family cash flow is channelled into an 'offset' account to minimise the non-deductible interest payable. From here an agreed monthly amount for living is transferred to an 'everyday' or cost of living account, and everything to do with household living expenses settles back with this account. Other planned expenses like holidays and school fees come from the offset account as and when required.

The elegant simplicity of this approach is that it is so easy to stay accountable. By watching two accounts, the everyday account and the offset account, you very quickly see whether you are making progress or not. If the offset account is going up, (your mortgage is going down), you are making progress; if it is not, you have the opportunity to consider your trade-offs and alternatives.

A Positive Cash Flow Story

This story lies behind my passion for helping people get their household spending in order.

Before going into business in 1999 my family spent several years paying down personal debt to get into the position to be able to leave a well-paying job to commence a 'start-up'. While the first few years of business were better than planned, we kept things pretty lean and it wasn't until 2006 that we really began to be rewarded for all our effort and hard work.

Then came the GFC and an inevitable downturn in business. While our business fared well relative to the broader industry, we learned a valuable lesson that all business owners need to be reminded of from time to time, and that is that business owners get paid last.

To the outside world little changed, but behind the scenes the owners decided to take very significant pay cuts (read 100%) to preserve the company's capital, preparing for the possibility that we might face a long, painful downturn.

On the home front, we accepted this reality and simply implemented a new policy: If we didn't have the money, we couldn't spend it. Sounds old fashioned, but it worked.

First, credit cards were put away and we began living off debit cards. We then implemented the cash flow plan you see in Figure 11, meaning that we lived off a fixed amount each month and ensured we made ends meet. We still planned for holidays and other treats but lived within our means. The funny thing was that while cash flow reduced, our lifestyle remained largely unchanged.

The changes we made were liberating, as we always knew where we stood financially and it created a positive conversation in the household around our financial priorities. Each month we either have month left at the end of the money, or money left at the end of the month.

Credit cards

We have seen families where there is almost an addiction to reward or frequent flyer points and therefore the spending needed to accumulate them. But the problem with credit cards is that they are designed to have you spend as much as possible without any real sense of the total amount being spent until the statement arrives at the end of the month. The more you spend, the more the card provider makes in transaction fees, so be in no doubt that their motivation is to have you spend more.

The use of credit cards is fine if you have an unlimited spending budget, but extreme care is needed when there is a cap on the amount your family can afford to spend. With credit card interest rates close to 20 per cent per annum, any outstanding balance will be a significant drag on your financial progress.

By transitioning away from the use of credit cards for living expenses you can change the money conversation in your family. By using debit cards instead, more conscious thought is given to what you are spending during the month and as the month draws to a close there may even be a conversation about deferring spending until the following month.

Debt management

Debt can be very effective in improving your asset base by allowing you to leverage into growing assets. However, over-indebtedness is one of the fastest ways to undermine wealth. Structure your debt effectively and have a plan to reduce debt in a timely way and it will be possible to achieve financial security many years before you might have otherwise.

We see families that have both deductible and non-deductible debt and an equal focus on the repayment of both. Our advice is to restructure payments to clear the non-deductible loans first, while benefiting from the tax effectiveness of the deductible debt. A simple restructure like this can save thousands of dollars in tax and hasten the repayment of debt.

What's more, banking in Australia is very competitive and it may not pay you to be too loyal to your bank. It is common for the best deals to be offered to new customers while loyal long-term customers languish in older, higher rate products. As a commercial organisation your bank probably isn't going to volunteer a lower rate unless you ask, but it is possible to achieve annual savings in the thousands of dollars by doing so – or by getting a better deal elsewhere.

Managing tax

People get busy, so it is easy to overlook tax planning and the benefits it can offer. It is true that the tax system has become tighter in recent years, but this is only more reason to ensure you claim every benefit to which you are entitled and to maximise every available deduction.

If you're employed, tax is relatively straightforward because you pay at source. But for some other professionals and for business owners the planning opportunities can be considerable.

For doctors, lawyers and other self-employed people, managing tax is critical. The nature of the pay-as-you-go system in Australia means you need a plan and a structure to ensure your tax remittances are set aside and paid at the due date. The most effective way to handle future tax liabilities can be to use loan offset accounts set against non-deductible debt.

The bottom line is you must stay on top of your taxes. Keep good records of potential deductions and file your returns promptly each year. You don't want a black mark with the Tax Office and you don't want back taxes building up.

Practical ways of saving tax

- Never hold a credit balance in an interest bearing account when it could be offsetting non-deductible debt.

- Place interest bearing accounts in the name of family members on the lowest tax rate.

- Pay off non-deductible debt first.

- Maximise your use of superannuation, both concessional and non-concessional contribution limits.

- Claim depreciation and amortisation on investment property.

- Consider the best tax entity to use before you invest (we look at this below).

- Structure business assets to take advantage of small business capital gains tax (CGT) rollover relief.

- Use a company beneficiary to receive trust distributions.

Tax on your investments

Most investors don't even contemplate the tax they pay on their investment portfolio because to a large degree it is beyond their control. If you trade shares or invest in highly traded managed funds your tax liability will be far higher than if you use a buy-and-hold strategy for quality assets. Traded portfolios, including hedge funds, create many more transactions and, to the extent they are profitable, result in taxable income or taxable capital gains. Investments held in discretionary trusts pay tax at the beneficiaries' marginal rate while superannuation funds pay tax at 15 per cent.

Most money managers, including stockbrokers, are not tax aware because it makes little difference to their bottom line. But savvy investors can considerably improve their investment outcomes by managing turnover effectively.

Using entities to manage tax

Superannuation remains an extraordinarily generous structure. It offers tax-deductible contributions, a low tax rate in the savings phase and very generous tax concessions in retirement. While it is common to hear complaints about the system continually changing, there are still good reasons to embrace it.

If all other things remain equal – investment returns, savings rates and investment term – the only other variable is tax. Compare superannuation on this basis with any other structure and it wins hands down. Yes, you are locking savings away for the long term, but the benefits of superannuation should place this structure squarely at the centre of your strategic plan.

Discretionary family trusts are also a very effective ownership structure, particularly when you have business interests that pay fully franked dividends. Trusts allow you to split income across multiple beneficiaries, including adult children, parents, companies and charities.

Let's take the example of an income of $200,000 being paid to one person. Under normal circumstances the tax paid by the individual including the Medicare levy would be $67,632. If the same income of $200,000 were paid via trust distributions across four adult beneficiaries, in equal portions, the total tax paid would reduce to $34,188.

While the use of trusts needs to be considered very carefully, the long-term benefits can be considerable, particularly when they are part of a strategic plan. Benefits of trusts can include:

- Distribution of income to multiple beneficiaries, including companies;

- Protection of trust assets from legal claim; and,

- Passing control of assets across generations without crystallising CGT.

Companies are another entity to be considered when tax planning. Many families have cash in the form of retained profits in company structures, including company beneficiary structures. When buying investment assets the question is whether they should be purchased in the company's name, because of the lower corporate tax rate.

The alternative could be to invest in a trust using monies loaned from the company to the trust. This is a very complex area and one that needs advice, but it is increasingly common to use a company as an investment vehicle to limit the tax paid to the corporate rate. Additional tax is paid only when a dividend is made to individual shareholders, which may be many years into the future.

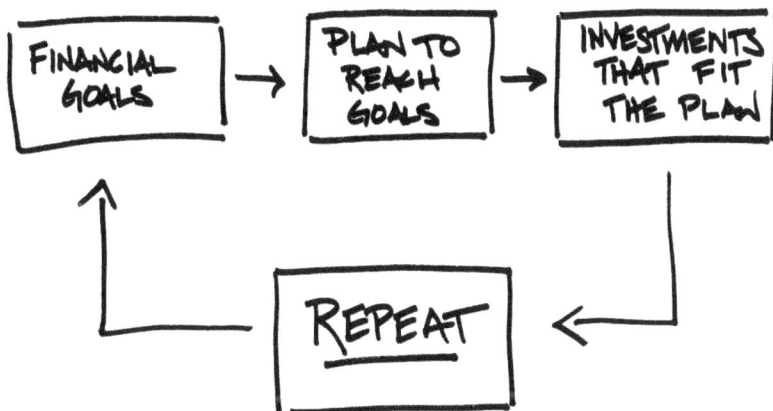

FINANCIAL GOALS → PLAN TO REACH GOALS → INVESTMENTS THAT FIT THE PLAN → REPEAT →

10. The Most Common Question: How Much is Enough?

"Wealth is the ability to fully experience life."

Henry David Thoreau

Do a Google search for 'safe withdrawal rates for retirees' and it will return more than 100 million results. So if you've been wondering how much is enough, you're not alone. Assuming that most of you don't plan to rely on the age pension, the question then is: How much is enough? It is a very important question to ask. But knowing how much is enough is not at all easy.

In attempting to answer this question we need to understand the inputs to the equation. These are nicely summarised as the five big questions:

1. How much can you save?

2. How much risk do you want to take?

3. How much money will you need to fund your future goals and lifestyle expenses?

4. When will you need to drawdown on your portfolio?

5. What do you want to leave behind?

THE 5 BIG QUESTIONS:
① HOW MUCH CAN YOU SAVE?
② HOW MUCH RISK?
③ HOW MUCH WILL YOU NEED?
④ WHEN WILL YOU NEED IT?
⑤ WHAT DO YOU WANT TO LEAVE?

FUTURE

PRESENT

For many years, finance researchers have suggested that drawing down 4 per cent of your portfolio a year is a safe withdrawal rate. If a retiree invested in a balanced portfolio and drew down 4 per cent of their portfolio each year they could reasonably expect their assets to last 30 years, the argument went. Using the 4 per cent rule, a retirement income of $100,000 a year would require capital at retirement of $2.5 million.

When considering how much is enough, we do need to consider the risk of 'portfolio ruin' – in other words, running out of money. And more recent Australian research suggests the 4 per cent rule may not be that safe at all.[8] Researchers Drew and Walk suggest that because Australia's investment returns have been the highest of any developed country for the past 100 years we may well be expecting too much in the future. If our returns are lower in the next 50 years than they were in the last 50, a drawdown rate of 4 per cent simply won't provide investors with enough certainty that their money will last the distance.

So, a slightly safer drawdown rate of 3.5 per cent annually would require closer to $2.9 million in starting capital to produce a retirement income of $100,000 a year.

With that insight into the most recent research, let's consider your position.

How much you need mainly depends on whether your strategy is 'drawdown driven' or 'legacy driven' and the length of time you will be drawing on your investment pool – the earlier you retire the larger your capital base needs to be, while continued work even on a part-time basis will stretch out your drawdown.

Drawdown-driven

Those of you who are drawdown-driven believe you are likely to consume much of your investment capital during your lifetime.

You will be looking out to a time horizon of 30 to 40 years in retirement and while you may have some regard for passing wealth to children and grandchildren this isn't your highest priority.

For those in the retirement or drawdown phase, the prospect of running out of money is usually the biggest concern. Managing your capital to minimise the possibility of errors and ensuring your wealth is not eroded by inflation become the two most important areas to consider.

Superannuation will probably be the ideal structure for you because the tax benefits are considerable and will stretch your wealth further.

As you move your superannuation into the pension phase you will be required to draw down a minimum of 4 per cent of your account each year and the level of drawdown will increase over your lifetime.

Most people with a reasonable level of wealth fit into this category and, to a large extent, the superannuation system in Australia is built around this notion.

Legacy-driven

Those of you who are legacy-driven expect to live off your capital during your lifetime before passing it on to your heirs. It is possible you are wealthier and have greater complexity around your structures. As a tax structure, superannuation remains attractive but much of your wealth is likely to be held in discretionary trusts and companies.

Drawdown levels become very important for legacy-driven investors and a target portfolio drawdown of 2 to 3 per cent a year increases the likelihood of preserving your capital. Your biggest concerns will be preserving the real value of your assets across generations, so inflation protection and spending rates become the key areas of focus.

You may also need to consider different investment strategies for different pots of money, to achieve specific objectives. This approach can take much of the worry out of your planning by identifying a pot of money to fund your lifestyle and then a separate pot to fund your legacy objectives. You may take fewer risks with the money you need to live off, while exposing the remaining assets to higher-risk investments that have a higher expected return.

1. Liability Matching Portfolio	2. Return Seeking Portfolio	3. Other Priorities
Conservatively designed and managed to maximise probability that core goal liabilities are met.	Funds are surplus to core goals. Seeks higher returns to fund additional goals and legacy priorities.	Business investments, Philanthropy etc.

Figure 12: Investment framework to manage risk

11. Lifetime Cash Flow Modelling

"My life didn't please me so I created my life"

Coco Chanel

Perhaps the most important part of the strategic planning process is the financial modelling that shows exactly where you are, how close that is to where you want to be, and what you might need to do to achieve the outcomes you desire.

The *Lifetime Cash Flow Model* paints a very clear picture of how achievable your goals are and what trade-offs might be needed. Far from daunting, in our experience this can be liberating. The modelling often provides the clarity people need to start making smarter decisions. In a practical way, it underpins the step-by-step plan of everything that needs to be done.

The important inputs into your financial model will be:

- Starting capital and annual savings rates;

- Current tax structures, (superannuation, trusts, companies);

- Your capacity for investment risk;

- Future investment return estimates;

- Future inflation estimates;

- Life expectancy;

- Future spending plans; and,

- Timing of funding of large goals.

There is an intrinsic value to creating a *Lifetime Cash Flow Model* that can't be underestimated. Once your base case scenario is created you will be in a position to assess just how well you are tracking towards your preferred outcomes.

Being well on track can give rise to inspiring conversations about the other things you might consider doing, such as ceasing work earlier, helping children enter the property market, travel, charitable giving and so on. Where your numbers don't quite add up, the lifetime model will create conversation about what trade-offs might be possible to get you back on track as early as possible.

Either way, a number of different options will flow out of the base case scenario. You can then move the dials, questioning and testing the different options available to you.

Of course, as with any long-term model, there is less certainty the longer out the model goes, but this uncertainty is managed by continuously monitoring your progress and, where necessary, resetting the model based on new information.

Let's look at an example to see how this might work for you. In this simple example John and Mary are considering their options for retirement. John is very happy to continue working into his late 60s but wants to continue working out of choice, not because he needs to.

Scenario 1 is their *base* case. It incorporates continued savings of $120,000 a year until age 63, after which an annual pre-tax income of $225,000 is drawn from the portfolio. The investment risk the family is comfortable with indicates a relatively low risk approach. In addition, we incorporate a gift of $250,000 to each of their adult

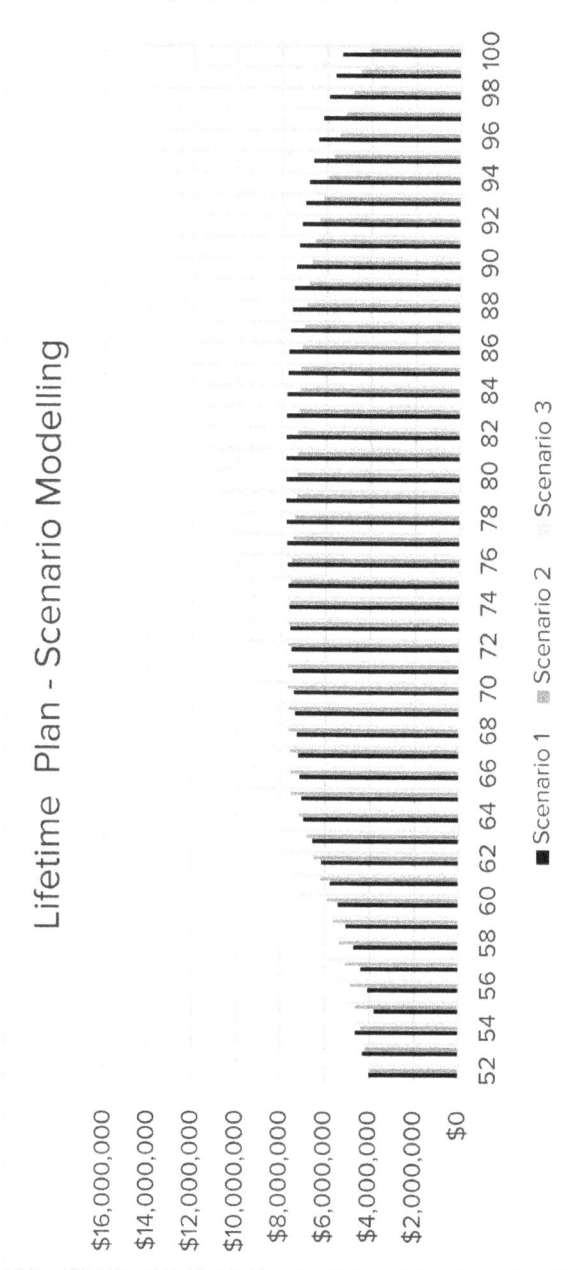

Figure 13: Lifetime plan – scenario modelling

children to help them buy homes of their own. In this scenario, the gifting occurs at about age 55, which is a very early and a large drawdown on capital.

As we review the results of this scenario, there is a slight diminution of capital in the later years of life. Depending on the legacy priorities of the family, this may be a perfectly acceptable outcome.

Scenario 2 begins to incorporate some of the results of John and Mary's pre-retirement discussions. The first big change is that John wants to see the impact of him reducing his work to three days a week up to age 65. This means no additional savings in the 13 years up to age 65. At age 65, they begin to draw down on the portfolio but instead of giving their children a lump sum gift they look at drawing down an additional amount each year for 15 years. Otherwise their lifestyle spending remains the same in Scenarios 1 and 2. To compensate for the reduction in savings, John and Mary decide to invest in a slightly riskier portfolio with expectation of a higher return.

As Scenario 2 unfolds we see that capital is eroded in the later years. While Scenario 2 may give John his ideal lifestyle in the early years, through part-time work, there may be considerable discomfort later as inflation and unexpected events impact the remaining capital base. Scenario 2 leaves little room for error and a market downturn at an inopportune time could seriously undermine their capital base.

Scenario 3 sees John and Mary decide to combine elements of both scenarios. They plan to gift lump sums to their children but not until retirement at age 65. They figure that having to wait 10 years will be beneficial for their children, encouraging them to work harder to establish themselves. John also elects to continue working full-time until retirement so their savings can be maximised. They also incorporate the slightly higher investment risk used in Scenario

2, deciding that while the additional investment risk will probably create short-term concerns during volatile markets, the likelihood of leaving a meaningful estate is greatly increased. So is the likelihood that future income and capital will be protected from inflation risk.

While none of these scenarios presents the 'right' answer the process is valuable in providing an evidence-based approach to decision-making, trade-offs and uncertainty.

Enhancement

With greater clarity comes opportunity, and the next step in the strategic planning process is to assess how to get the best possible outcome. This is often referred to as *Advanced Planning* and involves an assessment of tax considerations, asset ownership, structuring and future planning – all designed to deliver the most efficient outcome possible.

Depending on the complexity of your affairs, the enhancement process may need the input of different kinds of expertise from tax, accounting and legal specialties. The right network of advisers can add considerable value to the enhancement process through efficiencies and savings in one form or another. For wealthier families the impact can be substantial. Some of the considerations taken into account in enhancement will include:

- Use of superannuation;

- Effective structures for ownership of assets;

- Remuneration structures;

- Business sale tax exemptions;

- Use of trusts;

- Tax planning; and,

- Asset protection.

You might think of enhancement as the fine-tuning that goes into your strategic plan to achieve the best possible outcome with the resources you have.

Taking care with financial models

When building financial models, many people take an overly simplistic view. Free online retirement calculators rely on 'straight-line' modelling, which can often provide investors with a false sense of security. The problem with straight-line models is that they assume a consistent annual return each year, and if there is one thing we know in the world of finance it is that financial markets are unpredictable.

Let's say you choose to model your portfolio with an assumed return of 8 per cent a year. That's close to the historical balanced fund return for the past 30 years, so what's the problem?

First, past returns are not a reliable proxy for future returns. The past 30 years have given us relatively high returns compared with the long-term average and it may be dangerous to expect these returns to continue. Next is the variability of investment markets, where each year delivers a result that could fluctuate significantly from the annualised return.

Straight-line models like our scenarios for John and Mary earlier, are great for narrowing down your different options, but once you have done that it's best to employ some more sophisticated modelling to stress test your strategy. One of the common stress tests is the Monte Carlo simulation. In these simulations we apply a random sample of future expected returns and historic returns to provide a range of possible outcomes depending on different economic scenarios and the level of confidence you want to have in the outcome. If your model has 1,000 simulations and 500 of them result in you having surplus capital at the end of the period, you would conclude that the current strategy has a 50 per cent chance of success; conversely there is a 50 per cent chance you will run out of capital during your lifetime.

Having tested the strategy, you should consider the results in terms of your level of confidence of a successful outcome. To increase your confidence level, you need to consider factors that include your annual spending, the timing of large capital withdrawals, your saving rate before retirement and the number of years you work before you retire. From our experience, relatively small reductions in annual spending over a long period of time can dramatically increase the level of confidence, as can working longer.

This is an area in which a financial professional trained to a fiduciary standard can provide you with considerable insight and confidence. Whether you choose to work with a financial professional or go it alone, this is an area that needs annual review to ensure your strategic plan remains sustainable.

12. Dealing with a Liquidity Event

"All I ask is the chance to prove that money can't make me happy."

Spike Milligan

Liquidity events present specific issues an individual may never have had to deal with before. Liquidity events fall into three broad categories and include the sale of a business or major asset, inheritance and divorce settlement. While each of these scenarios is quite different, common threads run through them. The first is that the event is likely to be a once in a lifetime occurrence and the recipient of the funds may not be prepared for what lies ahead.

Business sale

Many business owners are savvy with money and know exactly what to do when the proceeds of their business sale arrive, while others – having spent years focusing their energy on the growth of their business – are at a loss to know what comes next.

A study by *The Economist*[9] found that a majority of families who sold businesses felt a sense of loss in the years after the sale. One moment the business owner is fully engaged, the next they are searching around for something to occupy their time.

Planning a business sale well in advance and gaining the right advice along the way is important, but so is planning what to do after the sale. There's only so much golf anyone can play. Having interests and a focus post-sale become a major issue.

As for the sale process:

Get the right people involved – Your first port of call should be your accountant or business adviser. In some cases your accountant may not be in a position to advise you because the sale of a business is not their area of expertise. Find an adviser who has this experience and who is up to date with CGT matters.

Next you need an experienced commercial lawyer to work with your accountant to ensure property and legal issues are dealt with properly. The right sale agreement will ensure you get all the tax breaks you are entitled to.

As a key consideration, you will need to make sure your assumptions about how much money you will end up with after the sale are right. Ensuring your savings are adequate for the plans you have made is best done before the sale process begins.

Get the right tax advice in advance – The capital gain on the sale of a business asset is subject to tax but there are ways to maximise other tax benefits, particularly if yours is considered a small business. If you meet tax office guidelines you may be entitled to significant tax exemptions.

Getting these exemptions right may result in a tax-free business sale, but it is a complex area with many traps so make sure you get advice from a Chartered Accountant or CPA as early as possible.

While sound planning for your business sale will maximise your financial outcome, planning for life after the business sale will help ensure you enjoy the wealth you have released.

Inheritance

Inheritance can be very complicated and, depending on your family's circumstances, the amount of your inheritance can be a real shock. Parents born in the 1930s have very different attitudes towards money and for many it is a subject that simply isn't discussed in polite company. As a result when the inheritance does come through, the size can be something of a surprise to the recipients.

This situation is more pronounced when the recipient has lived a perfectly normal life, worked hard, paid off loans and done all the other normal things that normal people do. For these people, receiving a large inheritance can be quite challenging. On the one hand they may have feelings of gratitude to have received a sum that could be life changing, but there may also be emotion around how to deal with the money. When it means a new level of wealth, an inheritance needs to be dealt with differently.

The way you deal with your inheritance will principally depend on the size of the inheritance and how wealthy you were before you received it. If you are already wealthy, the additional money may serve only to maintain and reinforce your current standard of living. It is likely you will already be experienced with money and will be well positioned to make the right decisions.

When the inheritance is significant or represents newfound wealth, it is common for recipients to feel a real weight of responsibility to make the right decisions and to steward the money responsibly. If you have never had the experience of managing a large sum of money before, it is common to feel completely unprepared for this responsibility.

In these circumstances wealth planning needs to be thorough and incorporate a large education component, to ensure the inheritor has the financial skills they need to feel in control.

It is rare that inheritors go it alone. Trust will be the main currency when choosing an adviser. Most people understand there will only be one opportunity to get the planning right.

Divorce settlements

The process leading up to a divorce settlement represents an extraordinarily difficult period in anyone's life. Regardless of who initiates it, divorce involves intense emotions, potentially including anger and sadness.[10] Financial settlements are particularly difficult for women if they have not been the main income earner in the family, and even harder when the woman has had little input into or knowledge of the family's finances.

Divorce lawyers report that professional advisers such as the family accountant, faced with a relationship breakdown, almost always retain their relationship with the husband, who is perceived to represent the better long-term business opportunity.[11]

In Australia, the trend has been for the Family Court to move away from 'maintenance' orders and it is now increasingly common for divorce settlements to involve a 'clean break' settlement.

These factors leave women in particular in a difficult position. Not only are they seeking to build a new life but they also need a plan for their financial settlement so it is employed as effectively as possible. In research conducted by my business partner Chris King, four recurring themes became apparent when divorcing women discussed their financial challenges.[12] These themes include lack of knowledge of the family's affairs; the overwhelming complexity of having to build a financial plan from scratch; no source of income; and the newfound responsibility for the future.

As the settlement nears, the need to look forward and contemplate a new financial future becomes real. Approaching this new chapter of life with confidence requires an open mind, a willingness to tackle new things and a commitment to taking control.

In taking control, you will need to appoint a new accountant and potentially a new financial adviser. The section entitled *Working with a Financial Professional* may assist.

13. Monitoring Progress

"Success is 10 per cent Inspiration, and 90 per cent Perspiration."

Thomas Edison

Once you have a strategic plan, conducting a regular progress update is arguably the most important thing you can do. Many financial advisers offer a portfolio review service to see how investments have performed in the past year, but it is not enough just to review investments.

Monitoring your progress should start with a review of your goals and priorities. Have they changed? Are you still committed to them in the same way you were?

Then there's the broader context of your life. Has something happened in the family or extended family to disrupt your progress? Is your spending still on track? Are you saving as you should be?

From here you will need to review every aspect of your strategy to ensure your financial house is still in order. Using the comprehensive wealth management model I have outlined, you will have the step-by-step approach you need to guide you through the process of ensuring that everything is as it should be.

In Figure 14 we present a real example of a family's progress report, where we plot their progress periodically since 2004. In this report we have excluded the value of the family home on the basis that they will always need a roof over their heads, so the starting position is a relatively small pot of savings to invest.

What unfolds is a picture of regular and disciplined saving and investing, with a real focus on the achievement of the goals that are important to them. In the graph we measure three things. First we measure the family's total investment asset position – the sum of all their investment assets. We then measure the family's total debt position. Finally, by deducting the total debt from the total investment assets, we are left with their net asset position. Ultimately, it is your net asset position that will fund your goals.

Looking at the seeming lack of progress in the early years, it is easy to see how people can become disenchanted, and this is when commitment can wane. Yet if we look over a longer period we can see the remarkable progress this family has made. The key benefit of monitoring progress in this way is that a long-term picture emerges of the results of all the positive financial decisions they made each day. If we look at the trends, we see two key indicators of success. The first is the gradual but steady increase in investment assets, and the second is the gradual reduction in outstanding debt.

Incremental improvements in these two measures over time combine to create a picture of success that most people would be happy to emulate.

Achieving enduring financial success is not easy, but by having a clear sense of direction, the right strategy to get you there and an effective method of keeping score you will be well on your way to achieving the success to which you aspire.

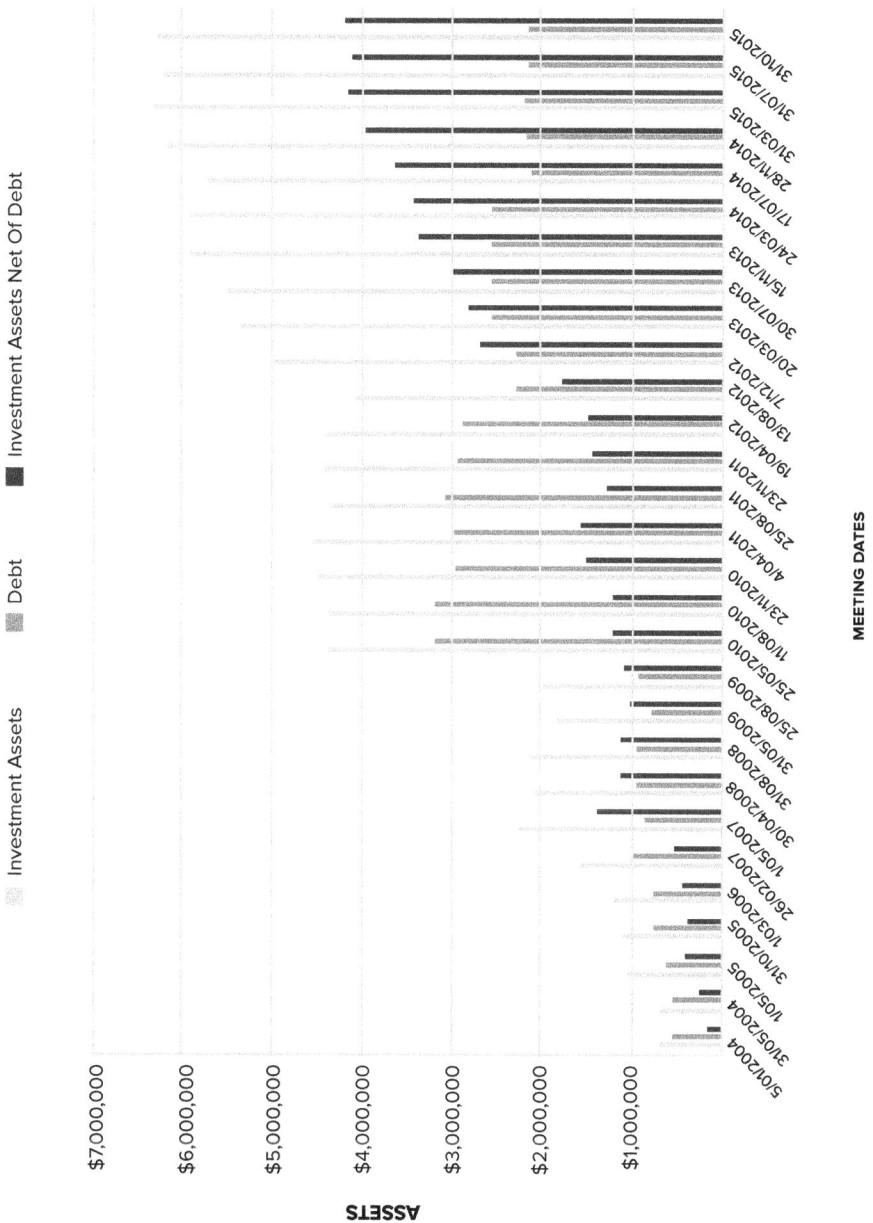

Figure 14: Progress report

Net Worth Statement | David and Mary Jones | As at May 2016

Personal Assets		Asset	Liability
Joint Assets			
Family Home		$1,500,000	
Total		**$1,500,000**	

Investment Assets		Asset	Liability
David Jones			
Employer Superannuation		$6,000	
Rental Property Cash Account		$27,500	
Superannuation Portfolio		$846,600	
Investment Property		$1,200,000	$850,000
	Sub-Total	**$2,080,100**	**$850,000**
Mary Jones			
Holiday Home		$730,000	$350,000
Business Account		$42,200	
Holiday Home offset account		$350,000	
Superannuation Portfolio		$290,700	
	Sub-Total	**$1,412,900**	**$350,000**
Joint Investments			
Everyday Account		$3,500	
Short Term Savings		$8,200	
	Sub-Total	**$11,700**	
Jones Family Trust			
Shares in ASX Companies		$150,000	
Investment Portfolio		$1,500,900	
	Sub-Total	**$1,650,900**	
Total		**$5,155,600**	**$1,200,000**
Investment Assets less Total Liabilities		**$3,955,600**	
Total Assets (including Personal Assets)		**$6,655,600**	
Net Asset Position (Total Assets less Total Liabilities)		**$5,455,600**	

Figure 15: Family net worth statement

Section Take-outs

....

....

....

....

....

....

....

....

....

....

PART III

INVESTMENT PLANNING

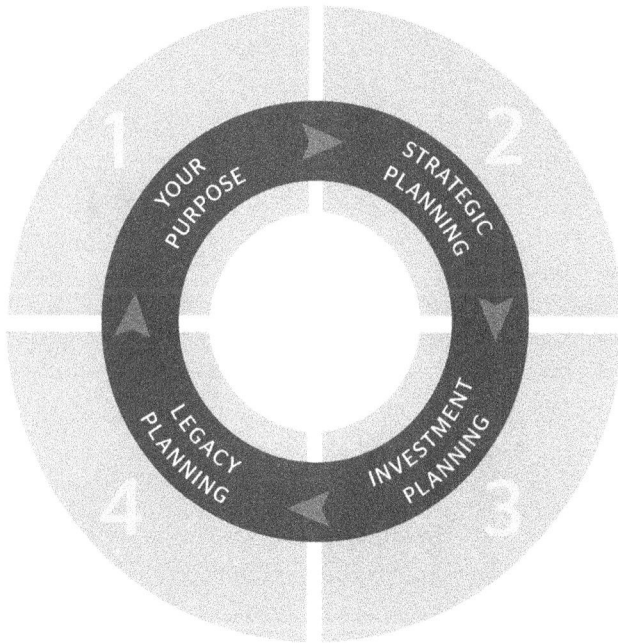

14. Getting the Investment Returns You Deserve

"We have long felt that the only value of stock forecasters is to make fortune-tellers look good."

Warren Buffett

Having taken the time to develop your *Purpose* and your *Strategic Plan*, you have now arrived at the point of implementing the investments that will underpin your long-term plan. Many may view this next stage, *Investment Planning*, as the 'fun part' – indeed, a lot of people mistakenly start here, ignoring the first two steps in the process altogether.

Of all the mistakes we see people make in their financial planning, the biggest are in the areas of tax and investing. Unfortunately, a significant error of judgment in either of these areas can be irreversible and very difficult to recover from.

This section will walk you through the steps you need to take to build a robust investment plan based on a tried and tested investment methodology. We will also look at the investment and behavioural pitfalls you would do well to avoid.

Warren Buffett is probably the most renowned investor of our time and he advocates that investors without specialist investment expertise of their own should have a significant proportion of their wealth in a portfolio of diversified shares. Yet many investors are anxious about the share market because of the periods of volatility we go through from time to time.

But if we look at our alternatives we quickly see that investing in cash is not the best or safest alternative. Cash is often referred to as a 'risk-free' asset, but while we all enjoy the feeling of security from having money in the bank, cash is unlikely to fund our long-term security.

In a landmark study of investment returns, UK-based Professor Elroy Dimson led a team of researchers that reconstructed over 100 years of asset class data for most of the developed countries in the world. [13] Using this data we can see the value of $100 invested in cash and $100 invested in Australian shares over the past 110 years, after adjusting for inflation. In real terms the cash investment barely doubles in value, while the share investment grows many times.

Value of $100 invested for the last 100 years
Values shown are above inflation ie. "real returns"

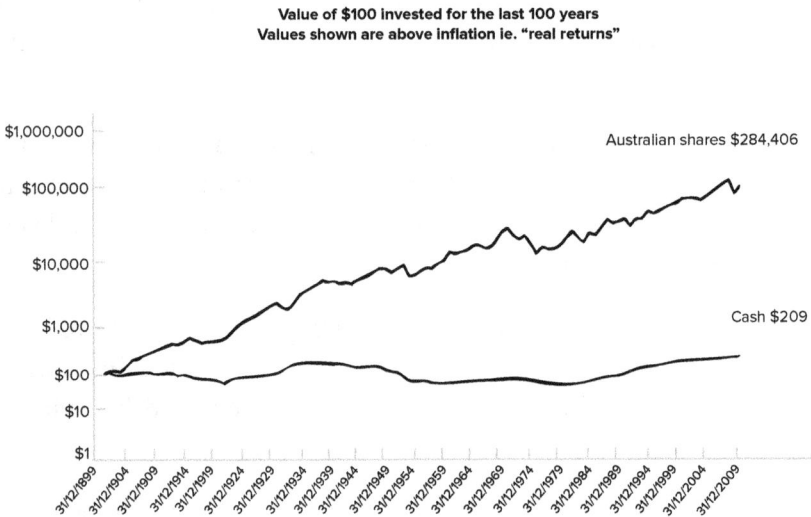

Source calculated by MLC using data presented in DMS Data Module offered through the Morningstart software program EnCorr. Based on copyrighted books by Dimson Marsh and Staunton Triumph of the Ophmists Princeton University Press (c) 2002 and Global Investment Returns Yearbook 2003 ABN AMRO/London Business School (c) 2003. All rights reserved. Used with permission.

Figure 16: Real returns cash vs. shares[14]

Inflation is one of the great challenges for investors over their lifetimes. How can we grow our investment assets in real terms without exposing our money to unnecessary risk? This is where the question of risk and investing becomes a little complicated. It comes down to one simple question: would you rather eat well, or sleep well? From an investment perspective, the idea of *sleeping well* may mean keeping things very safe and avoiding market ups and downs by having less of what you might consider riskier assets. But do this and there's a different risk – the increased likelihood that the purchasing power of your investments will be significantly degraded by inflation.

To illustrate the effect of inflation over time, let's look at the price of milk. Back in 1913, just 9 cents would have purchased a litre of milk. By 1963, it would have purchased a small glassful. By 2015, inflation has eroded your purchasing power to such an extent that 9 cents bought you just 6 tablespoons of milk.[15]

1913	1963	2015

$0.09 = 1 Litre	$0.09 = 1 Small Glass	$0.09 = 6 Tablespoons

Figure 17: Impact of inflation on spending (1913-2015)

So, if you are to maintain the real value of your capital, it will be necessary to expose your portfolio to some uncertainty. How you go about doing this will determine the ultimate success of your investing.

The power of markets

It was back in 1776 that Scottish philosopher Adam Smith published the *Wealth of Nations*, in which he outlined the ideal basis for a free market system that creates wealth and underpins prosperity. This included the division of labour, competition, the profit motive and free flow of knowledge.

While capitalism as we know it today may not be a perfect system, it is a very effective and efficient method of allocating and generating wealth. It is certainly the best system we have available to us at the present time.

At the core of capital allocation is the concept of risk and return. Each time an investor seeks to allocate their capital they assess the risks of the investment against the expected return.

When capital is allocated via the stock market investors have many choices around which companies to invest in, with each company presenting differing risks and expected returns. Companies compete for capital and millions of investors compete for access to the most attractive returns. In developed markets, investors have a reasonable expectation that the financial system is properly regulated, transparent and that pricing and settlement of securities is efficient and free from interference.

Since January 1926, until time of writing, the US share market has delivered an average compound return of 9.77 per cent a year.[16] In other words, one dollar invested in 1926 would have grown to $4,384 in that time.

So I propose that what an investor really needs to do in order to achieve a good investment outcome, is save regularly, keep costs low, take a long-term view and then, most importantly, efficiently capture the returns capitalism has on offer.

How business raises capital

All businesses need capital to operate effectively. Working capital funds day-to-day operations, while longer-term capital is needed to build plant and buy equipment. To fund these activities, businesses need to access the pool of money available from investors.

For privately owned businesses, capital is provided by the company's shareholders and, if borrowings are necessary, by their banks.

For public companies, the pool of available capital is larger and includes the stock market and bond market. When a public company needs to raise funds it will raise share capital from investors (shareholders) or borrow money from a bank or investors (bondholder).

Figure 18: Capital raising for companies via shares or bonds

Stock market

The stock market refers to the exchanges around the world where buyers and sellers trade existing shares in a company. The market provides a way for shares to efficiently change hands and for investors to access liquidity and discover prices. A transaction always involves two parties – a buyer and a seller – and these parties usually have different views of the company's profit outlook.

As with any free market, share prices are influenced by expectations and demand. You could view a company's share price as reflecting the consensus view of all buyers and sellers in the market. In 2015 global share markets averaged 98.6 million trades a day valued at A$447.3 billion per day.[17] These numbers confirm the idea that markets are enormous information processors, assimilating new information into prices moment by moment.

According to financial theory, a company's share price is determined by three factors:

a. Expected company earnings (dividends);

b. The expected rate of return; and,

c. The expected earnings growth rate.

As new information arises, buyers and sellers make judgments about how the news will affect a company's future earnings and risk. Market forces move the share price to reflect the aggregate opinions of all market participants. For example, if new information indicates that a company's earnings will be higher than expected in the next period, investors will most likely bid up the share price to match their new expectation. The expected rate of return increases only when the share appears to be getting riskier to own.

Bond market

Bonds are also known as fixed interest securities. They are issued by governments and government-backed organisations, along with companies. Most governments issue bonds to fund their operations or spending on major infrastructure, for example.

When a government or company issues a bond they are issuing a loan document that promises to repay the borrowed money at some agreed date in the future. There is usually an agreed rate of interest to be paid by the issuer to the lender at agreed intervals.

Bonds have financed government and private enterprise for centuries and traditionally have been regarded as less risky than shares because bond holders in most countries have a legal claim to a bond issuer's assets. Bond market volatility is generally lower than share market volatility. However, historically bonds have offered lower returns because bond holders do not participate in company profits or the appreciation in the company's share price.

According to financial theory, a bond price is determined by three factors:

a.   The creditworthiness of the bond issuer;

b.   The promised interest return on the bond; and,

c.   The length of time before the bond issuer is expected to repay the investor's capital.

While there is a vast array of different investment options to choose from, the share market and bond markets are most likely to underpin portfolio construction for most investors. For this reason it is important for investors to have confidence in these markets. Let's look at that next.

Are financial markets efficient?

The *Efficient Markets Hypothesis* is an important principle for understanding how markets work and what we should focus on as investors. When it comes to the best approach to investing, debate rages in the financial services industry between the evidence-based camp and the more speculative active management camp.

The *evidence-based* camp is comprised of the world's leading financial markets academics, several of whom have won the Nobel Prize for their contributions to financial markets research. In 1964 Professor Eugene Fama of The University of Chicago wrote his doctoral thesis on *The Behavior of Stock Market Prices*. In his thesis Fama, who has since become known as the 'father of modern finance', developed the Efficient Markets Hypothesis, which asserts that:

- Securities prices reflect all available information and expectations;

- Current prices are the best approximation of intrinsic value;

- Price changes are due to unforeseen events; and,

- Although shares may be mispriced at times, this condition is hard to recognise.

Viewing the markets as efficient has important implications. If current market prices offer the best available estimate of intrinsic value, stock mispricing should be regarded as a rare condition that cannot be systematically exploited through analysis and forecasting. Moreover, if new information is the main driver of prices, only unexpected events will trigger price changes. This may be one reason that share prices seem to behave randomly over the short term.

The Efficient Markets Hypothesis implies that it is difficult for an investor to consistently outperform the stock market except by chance. Market efficiency argues that when new information is available, market forces quickly push prices back towards a new fair value. No single investor can possibly have all the information needed to determine market prices as it will be scattered among many participants who are all competing to maximise their potential profit as buyers and sellers. The market mechanism gathers the information, evaluates it and builds it into prices.

Active fund managers believe exactly the opposite. They believe markets are inefficient and that they can routinely exploit market mispricing to gain a profit. This is almost the Holy Grail of investing and 'star' fund managers promote short-term performance as proof of their expertise. But perhaps the best test of market efficiency is the investment industry itself. In fact, active managers put market efficiency to the test every day as they research companies in a quest for mispricing. If market prices do not reflect fair value, the more skillful managers should be able to add value by finding mispriced shares and outsmarting other market participants consistently.

Each day around the world an enormous amount of effort goes into 'beating' the stock market in this way. Professional investors and mums and dads alike all search for the edge that will give them a better return. They believe that by picking the right shares, timing their entry in and exit out of the market correctly, they can 'win bigger' than the next person. While these efforts are well intentioned, the evidence suggests the reality is different, even when investors pay professional money managers to do the work for them.

There is a significant body of academic evidence suggesting managers who do beat the market, after fees, are more likely to do so as a result of chance, rather than skill.[18] Standard & Poor's conducts a survey[19] every six months to assess the effectiveness of active managers compared with their index manager counterparts and the overwhelming evidence is that very few fund managers can consistently beat the market on an after-fees basis. With the fees of active managers considerably higher than those of the alternatives, investors can be on an expensive pursuit of higher returns that often don't eventuate. The 2015 mid-year SPIVA Australia Scorecard, for instance, reports that 71 per cent of the 312 Australian large-cap managers failed to outperform the market over a five-year period.

This is not a one-off result as many surveys of this kind return such findings. But what if we could pick the 29 per cent of managers that do outperform? Unfortunately there is little persistence over time, with leading managers in one period falling back to the pack over time.

As the SPIVA research clearly shows, if professionals with vast resources cannot apply research and analysis to consistently pick winning shares it is even less likely that individuals can outperform the market.

Beware market gurus

This situation is also reflected in experts' opinions on the direction financial markets are headed. In the January 2008 edition of the Australian Financial Review's *Smart Investor* magazine, a group of experts published their predictions for the Australian share market over 2008.

Picking Stocks with Mary Sue

Every football fan who has entered a tipping contest has heard a story about the blissfully ignorant punter who won the competition by tossing a coin. For those who seriously follow the game it is perplexing to be beaten by a dabbler.

Well, you can imagine the reaction of the financial professionals competing to win $1 million in US TV network CNBC's stock picking contest when they heard that a waitress with no knowledge of the share market might take first prize.

Mary Sue Williams, a waitress for 20 years, was in 6th place in the final round of the 13-week competition on CNBC but stood to be elevated to first place because of trading irregularities by some of the leaders. (There's always someone trying to game the markets!)

To put this effort into context, this is a competition broadcast nationally in the US and attracting 375,000 contestants with 1.6 million virtual portfolios. Thousands of these people are financial professionals, stockbrokers and investment analysts with multiple university degrees, employing complex computer trading models.

Yet, a woman who had never bought or sold a stock in her life emerged from the pack to challenge the richly informed pros. Mary Sue works in an Italian restaurant overlooking an interstate freeway in a small town in Ohio. Her husband is a cook and neither spends any time fretting over share prices.

Asked by reporters to list the factors behind her rare stock picking skill, Mary Sue confided that it was a combination of gut feeling, common sense and "some eenie-meenie-minie-moe".

Cynicism aside, there are some simple lessons here for every investor.

Where we concentrate on capturing the returns of the asset classes that offer higher expected returns over the long term, we have won half the battle. Then by keeping costs low, managing the tax position of our portfolio and spreading our risk through diversification, our chances of matching or beating the professional money managers in the longer term are very high indeed.

7000 Is The Target In 2008

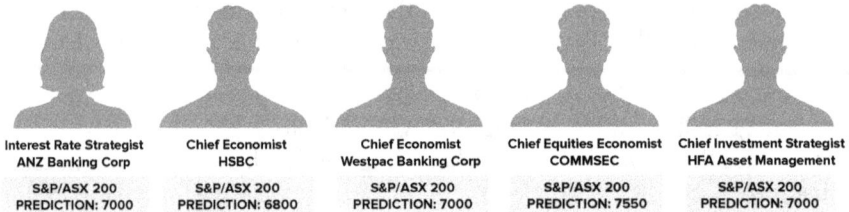

Interest Rate Strategist ANZ Banking Corp	Chief Economist HSBC	Chief Economist Westpac Banking Corp	Chief Equities Economist COMMSEC	Chief Investment Strategist HFA Asset Management
S&P/ASX 200 PREDICTION: 7000	S&P/ASX 200 PREDICTION: 6800	S&P/ASX 200 PREDICTION: 7000	S&P/ASX 200 PREDICTION: 7550	S&P/ASX 200 PREDICTION: 7000

Source: AFR Smart Investor, Jan 2008

Figure 19: Beware market gurus

The consensus was for the S&P/ASX 200 index to reach 7,000 points, representing a rise of 10.4 per cent. The index ended the year at 3,722 points, a fall of 41 per cent. Oops!

On 19 December 2011, respected journalist Alan Kohler announced on the ABC News that, "I believe the conditions are in place for another major panic sell-off on the share market ... on Monday I will be significantly reducing my already reduced exposure to equities to possibly zero."

The result of this dire prediction? Twelve months later the market had risen by just over 12 per cent.

Kohler was relying on his personal opinion on the possible outcome of future events, which by their very nature are uncontrollable. How can anyone factor into an assured forecast expectations of economic growth, corporate revenue in various sectors, employment and climactic occurrences, along with changes in government policy, international economic and political influences and investor psychology?

There are many examples like this, where market gurus simply get it wrong, with potentially disastrous effects for the investors who follow them. Fortunately, there is a better way.

If an investor believes securities are priced fairly, there is no longer any need to rely on market gurus. Rather than trying to outguess the financial markets, these smart investors let the markets work for them by continuously and efficiently targeting the dimensions of higher expected returns.

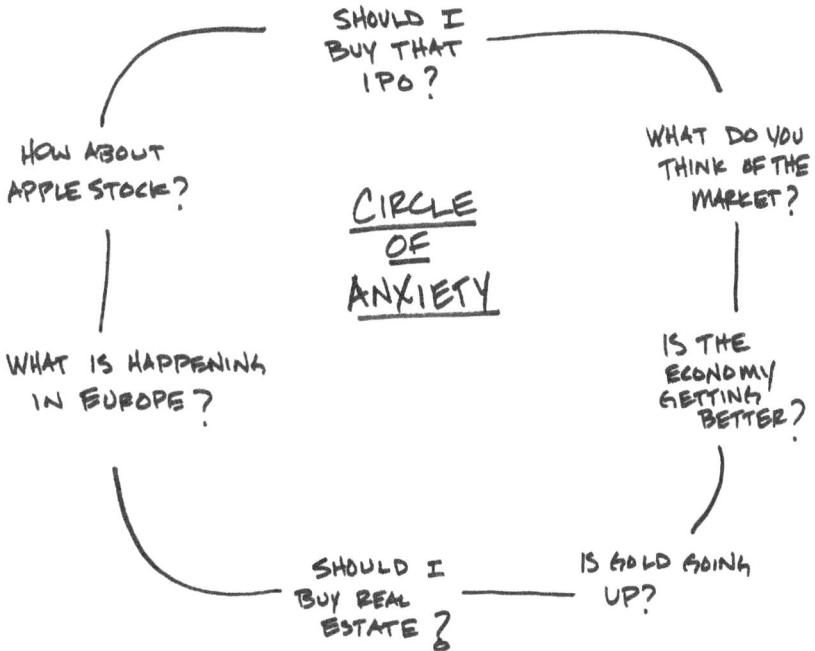

SHOULD I
BUY THAT
IPO?

HOW ABOUT
APPLE STOCK?

WHAT DO YOU
THINK OF THE
MARKET?

CIRCLE
OF
ANXIETY

WHAT IS HAPPENING
IN EUROPE?

IS THE
ECONOMY
GETTING
BETTER?

WHAT IS HAPPENING
IN EUROPE?

SHOULD I
BUY REAL
ESTATE?

IS GOLD GOING
UP?

15. Dimensions of Risk and Return Worth Targeting

"Whether we're talking about socks or stocks, I like buying quality merchandise when it is marked down."

Warren Buffett

Most investors intuitively understand that risk and return are related and that if you seek higher returns you will need to take some increased risk in the process. Figure 20 plots the value of one dollar invested in cash, diversified fixed interest and Australian shares since 1985. While the benefit of owning shares is clear to see in dollar terms, we also see that the road to achieving those returns is less predictable.

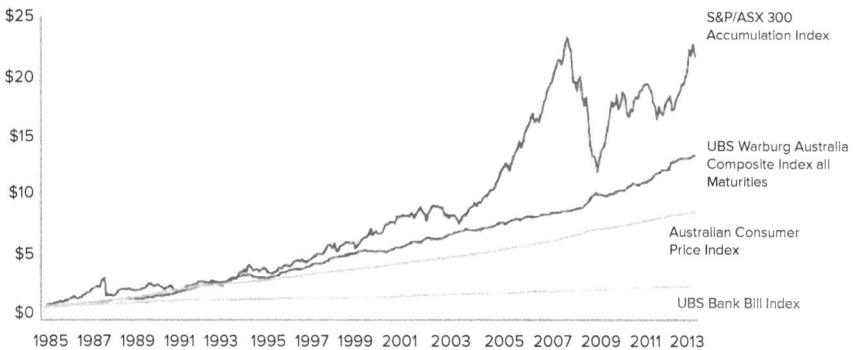

Figure 20: Growth of wealth – major asset classes

Risks worth taking

Investment risk can be measured many ways, including the possibility of fluctuation or loss in capital value. Research shows that there are some risks worth taking and some you should avoid.

Every share investment carries two types of general risk. The first is *stock-specific* risk, also known as non-systematic risk. This risk reflects the possibility that certain isolated events within a company or industry may affect that company's future profitability and share price. The most prominent example of this in the recent Australian context is the effect on iron ore companies – big and small – of the Chinese economic slowdown.

This stock-specific risk can be reduced through proper diversification in a portfolio. As such, it is also known as diversifiable or uncompensated risk. Investors are not paid an expected return to bear this risk because it can be managed through diversification.

Systematic risk is risk that relates to the whole share market. It reflects the broad conditions affecting all companies in the market or in an asset class. This risk cannot be diversified away. While we might prefer a smooth, easy investment ride we pay the price of the ups and downs of the market and in return receive a higher expected return on our investment. This risk is also known as market risk or compensated risk.

Around the world, academics and researchers continue to identify risks that are worth taking. In a landmark study Professor Eugene Fama of The University of Chicago and Professor Ken French of Dartmouth College[20] identified certain dimensions of stock market risk that are worth taking in pursuit of higher expected returns.

It is one thing to make a discovery in academia and another to be able to apply the research to an investor's portfolio. But with consistent research over many years, these dimensions have been found to be persistent over long periods and pervasive across all markets, providing the impetus for the financial industry to work out how these factors might be captured for the benefit of investors.

This school of thought is part of what is known as *Modern Portfolio Theory*. The remainder of this section outlines how the theory works and, more importantly, how you can use it to gain an investment edge.

Share market dimensions

Dimension 1: Market

Market risk simply refers to the risk of investing in the share market compared with the risk-free return on cash. This higher risk is compensated by a higher expected return for shares over cash and this premium is often referred to as the 'equity risk premium'. In the 35 years since January 1980, the S&P/ASX 300 accumulation index has provided an average annual compound return of 11.6 per cent, while for the same period Australian bank deposits have returned 8.7 per cent. The resulting market risk premium is reflected in the difference of 2.8 per cent. Over the period, $1 invested in shares would end up being worth $46, while $1 invested in cash would grow to $25.

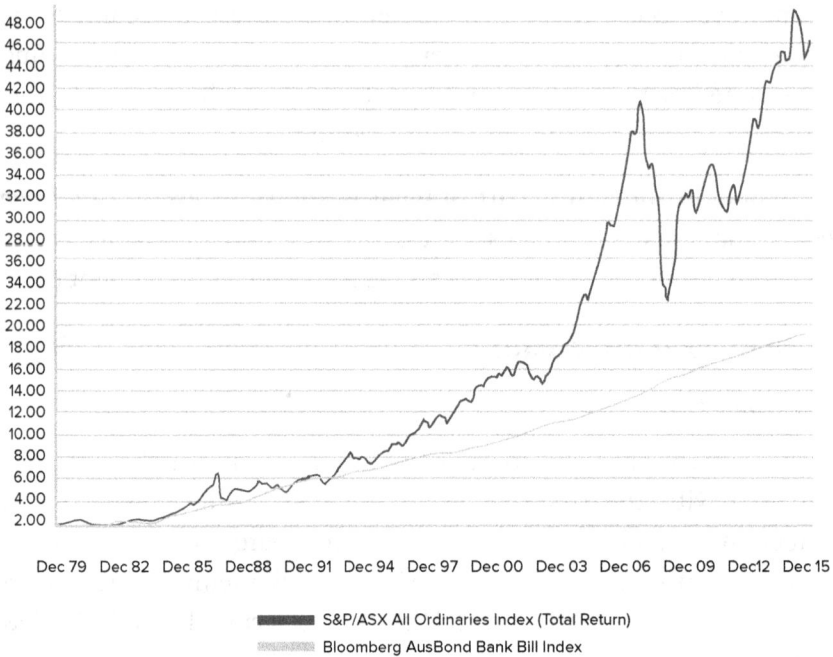

Dec 79	Dec 82	Dec 85	Dec88	Dec 91	Dec 94	Dec 97	Dec 00	Dec 03	Dec 06	Dec 09	Dec12	Dec 15

■■■■■ S&P/ASX All Ordinaries Index (Total Return)
▨▨▨▨ Bloomberg AusBond Bank Bill Index

Figure 21: Growth of wealth – market versus cash

We know that investing in shares will not reward you consistently each year and there will be periods in which your patience is tested. However, if we take a long-term view, the likelihood of being well rewarded is high. In overlapping 15-year periods since 1980 the share market has outperformed cash 93 per cent of the time. Over shorter periods the likelihood of cash outperforming the market increases, but the equity market remains the winner the majority of the time.

Overlapping Periods: January 1980-December 2015

Market beat Bank Bills

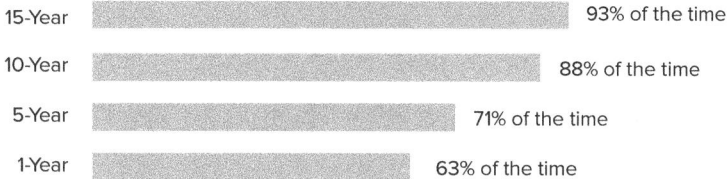

15-Year	93% of the time
10-Year	88% of the time
5-Year	71% of the time
1-Year	63% of the time

Figure 22: Share market versus cash[21]

An investment in the share market is the best way to gain exposure to the productive efforts of companies to innovate, grow and produce profits for shareholders. Every day we consume the goods and services produced by these companies and, as shareholders, we enjoy the rewards of their commercial success.

Dimension 2: Size

The size of the companies you invest in will also have a bearing on the return you receive. Larger companies, often household names, are considered safer while smaller companies we may have never heard of are often considered riskier. In the Australian context, Commonwealth Bank (ASX:CBA) is clearly a large company with a market capitalisation of $133 billion, while in comparison Bendigo and Adelaide bank (ASX:BEN) has a market capitalisation of $4.4 billion. In brewing and beverages, Lion Nathan (ASX:LNN) has a market capitalisation of $6.1 billion while brewing minnow Gage Roads (ASX:GRB) has a market capitalisation of $23 million. [22]

When it comes to raising capital, the larger companies compete with the smaller ones for investors' attention. Where there is higher perceived risk associated with the smaller company, investors will demand a higher return on their capital to compensate them for the higher risk . This makes perfect sense as larger, more secure companies will find it easier to raise capital, will have more established operations and will weather economic downturns more easily. As a result, investors receive a return commensurate with this more established position. For smaller companies, capital is more expensive to secure, investor scrutiny of their operations is higher and the risk of failure is greater. The resulting return profile is for higher returns but with higher risk of loss along the way.

This is best illustrated by taking a closer look at the relationship between risk and return in the combined US stock market. The Centre for Research in Securities Prices (CRSP) at The University of Chicago has reconstructed all US stock market data back to 1926. The centre ranks every stock listed on every exchange in the US by market capitalisation (size). The shares are then grouped into 10 equally numbered populations based on their size. As we see from Figure 23, CRSP-Decile 1 represents the largest companies, ranging up to CRSP Deciles 9 and 10 combined, representing the smallest companies. As we move out the size spectrum, from large to small, our return increases with each decile, as does our risk.

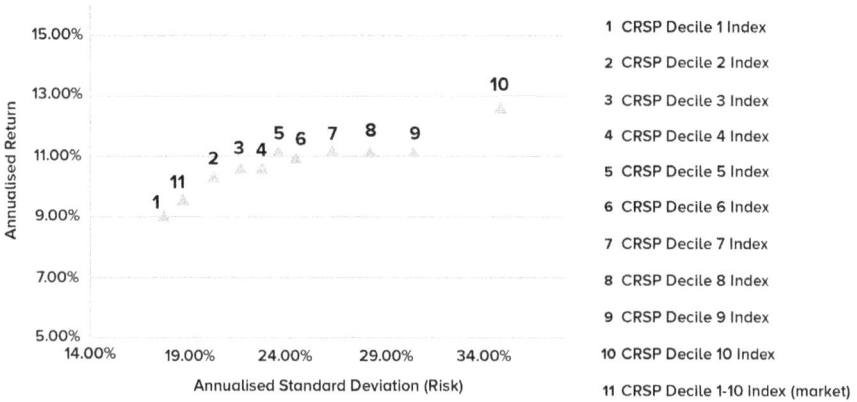

Figure 23: US Market, CRSP deciles 1-10.
(1 Jan, 1926 – 31 Dec, 2015)[24]

In Australia we also see the persistence of the small company premium over time, but it is important to be aware that the premium is not there all the time. Long periods can pass when larger companies outperform smaller companies. However, as Figure 24 illustrates, small has outperformed large 77 per cent of the time over rolling 15-year periods since 1974.

Overlapping Periods: January 1974-December 2015

Small beat Large

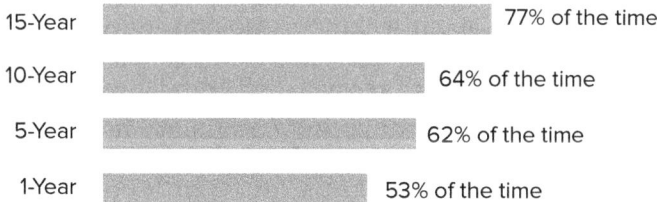

Figure 24: Australian small vs. large[25]

Dimension 3: Relative price

The third important dimension identified by Professors Fama and French is the contribution made by *value* stocks. Just as we can identify the difference between large and small companies, we can also identify differences between *growth* and *value* companies.

Growth companies are easy to define as those whose profits grow at a rate faster than other stocks in the market. Investors are willing to pay higher prices for growth stocks in the expectation of continued higher growth in profits and the perception of quality and security.

Conversely, value companies are less popular with investors and their relative prices are lower. The specific conditions contributing to what defines a value stock are difficult to pinpoint. But they are likely to have lower earnings growth and may have experienced management instability or a challenging business environment. These uncertainties increase risk. To be compensated for this higher risk investors expect to buy value stocks at larger discounts than the prices they are willing to pay for growth stocks.

An example of a value stock in recent times has been Qantas (ASX:QAN). After the financial crisis, Qantas struggled to be profitable amid competition from low-cost competitors, high fuel prices, a rising Australian dollar and overstaffing. As Figure 25 illustrates, Qantas was out of favour with investors for some years, leaving it significantly lagging the overall market. There were even questions at one point about whether it would survive.

From 2014, Qantas began to recover, helped by a falling Australian dollar, the benefits of restructuring, declining fuel charges and an easing of competitive pressures in the domestic market. The market recognised that a turnaround was under way and since then shareholders have enjoyed 250 per cent share price growth.

Figure 25: Qantas vs. all ordinaries index[26]

Like the small company premium, the value premium is transient. There can be long periods when value companies are out of favour and yet, as Figure 26 demonstrates, value investors have received significant rewards over time for the additional risks they take.

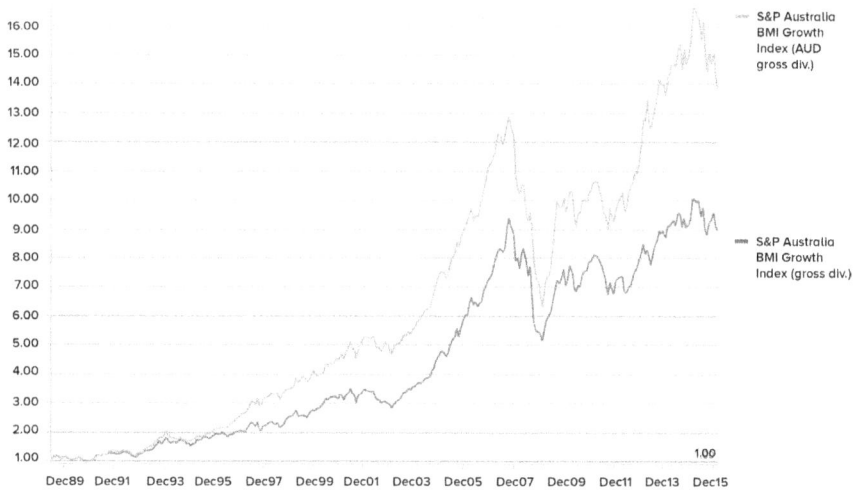

Figure 26: Growth of wealth - Value versus growth[27]

Since 1975 value companies have outperformed growth companies in every rolling 15-year period, in 89 per cent of rolling 10-year periods and in 79 per cent of rolling 5-year periods. We can't assume that value companies will outperform growth over every 15-year period in the future, so you will need to be patient, but investing in value stocks can make a big difference to the longer-term outcome you receive.

Overlapping Periods: January 1975-December 2015

Value beat Growth

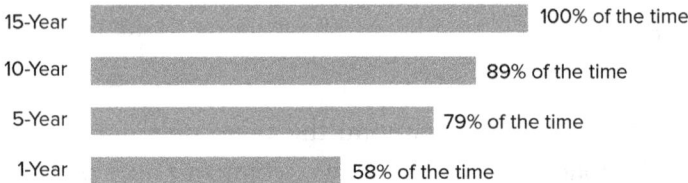

15-Year	100% of the time
10-Year	89% of the time
5-Year	79% of the time
1-Year	58% of the time

Figure 27: Value vs. growth[28]

Dimension 4: Direct profitability

For some time we have known that if two companies are trading at the same relative price, the one with higher expected profitability will have the higher expected returns. Warren Buffet is fond of saying that it is "far better to buy a wonderful business at a fair price than to buy a fair business at a wonderful price".

For many years, academics have searched for a reliable way to practically implement this knowledge in investment portfolios. A few years ago, Professor Robert Novy-Marx[29] of Rochester University identified profitability as a reliable source of higher expected return. This research has had important practical implications for portfolio construction as the profitability or *quality* dimension enables us to construct portfolios that favour companies displaying the attributes of higher expected return. This dimension is particularly valuable when it is applied in addition to the small and value company dimensions.

Overlapping Periods: January 1992-December 2015

High Profitability beat Low Profitability

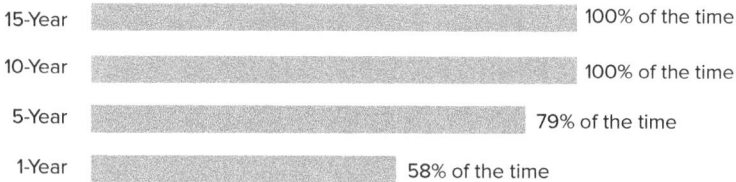

15-Year	100% of the time
10-Year	100% of the time
5-Year	79% of the time
1-Year	58% of the time

Figure 28: High profitability vs. low profitability[30]

The profitability dimension displays considerable persistence over 10-year and 15-year periods, with high profitability companies beating low profitability companies 100 per cent of the time. Over five-year and one-year periods, high profitability companies beat low profitability companies 89 per cent and 63 per cent of the time respectively. Again, the profitability dimension is not guaranteed but over longer periods, you should have a reasonable expectation of a higher expected return.

Bond market dimensions

The primary role of fixed interest or bond investments in your portfolio is to control risk. The secondary roles for fixed interest are capital protection and to provide an income return.

When we invest in bonds, outcomes are more predictable than in the share market and yet bond markets are not as well understood, even though they are many times larger than the world's share markets.

More often than not, the cash flow return from a bond is known so they are much easier to price than shares. The final two dimensions of higher expected return relate to bonds.

Dimension 5 – Credit risk

Credit quality is the primary indicator of the interest yield you will receive on a bond. Where credit quality is high the likelihood of your capital being returned at the end of the period is high, and so the income you receive along the way will reflect this. Generally speaking, bonds issued by the governments of developed countries like the US, Germany and Australia are considered very safe and investors have high levels of confidence in them. In contrast, a bond issued by a relatively unknown company will offer less security so, to attract investors, the return must be higher.

Dimension 6 – Term risk

Term risk refers to the fact that bonds that mature further into the future are subject to the risk of unexpected changes in interest rates. Unexpected increases in inflation can also affect the value of a bond with a longer maturity. Consequently, investors usually demand a higher yield (return) on longer-term bonds than on shorter-term bonds, though this is not always the case. At times of very low inflation and very stable interest rates, as we have seen in recent years, there has been less of a premium on long-term bonds. Indeed, in some cases, there has been a negative term premium.

What do the dimensions of return mean to you?

While many investors see building a portfolio as something of a guessing game, the identification of known dimensions of return that are persistent and pervasive has given us a far greater understanding of where premiums come from. The underlying and painstaking research into this over many decades has led to the awarding of several Nobel prizes.

So if the dimensions of return are so well known why doesn't everyone invest this way? Well, in fact large parts of the institutional investment sector *do* invest this way. For retail investors, though, there is the lure of the 'special sauce' that leads to higher returns and many large financial institutions have a vested interest in creating products that promise just that. And, of course, the more sophisticated they can make their products look, the better their marketing pitch and the wider their profit margins.

There is simply no financial incentive for most institutions to deliver low-cost, robust investment solutions because they get paid according to the volume of the investment transactions they create and the size of the management fee they can charge.

The good news for smaller investors is that being armed with knowledge of the dimensions of higher expected return gives you the information you need to build diversified, effective, robust and reliable investment portfolios based on sound evidence rather than on speculation.

Let's see how this works in more detail.

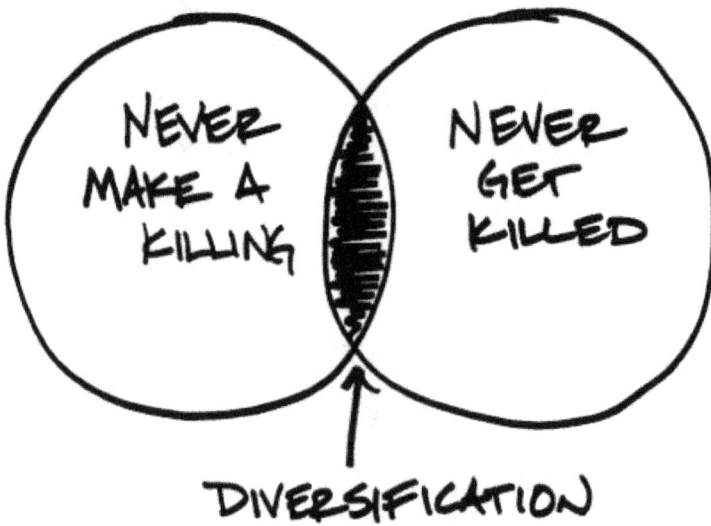

NEVER MAKE A KILLING — NEVER GET KILLED

DIVERSIFICATION

16. Risk and Asset Allocation

"To be alive at all involves some risk."

Harold MacMillan

As you begin to build your portfolio there are a number of key principles to consider, including how much risk you are prepared to take, how much return you need and how diversified the portfolio should be.

Investment risk

The first step in building your portfolio is to determine just how much risk you are prepared to take and what return is needed to fund your objectives. The moment you make the decision to invest in anything other than cash you are introducing uncertainty into your investment equation. The more you move away from cash the higher the uncertainty.

Many financial advisers will simply provide you with a questionnaire to determine your 'risk tolerance'. In many instances, your responses to the survey will drive the risk decisions in your portfolio. This approach is more about managing the advisers' business risk than your investment risk.

A better way to look at the risk decision is to consider these key areas:

1. **Risk required** – How much risk do you *need to take* to fund your long-term goals and to safeguard against inflation?

2. **Risk capacity** – How much risk can you *afford to take* without an unfavourable market event derailing your long-term plan?

3. **Risk tolerance** – How much risk do you *prefer to take* so that you have greater comfort in the investment process?

The level of return needed to fund your goals will be driven by the amount you need to draw down from your portfolio, the time when the drawdowns will commence, the extent of your existing capital and your savings rate, among other factors. Once you have taken these factors into account, and you need a return greater than the risk-free or cash return, your next step is to explore the sources of higher return.

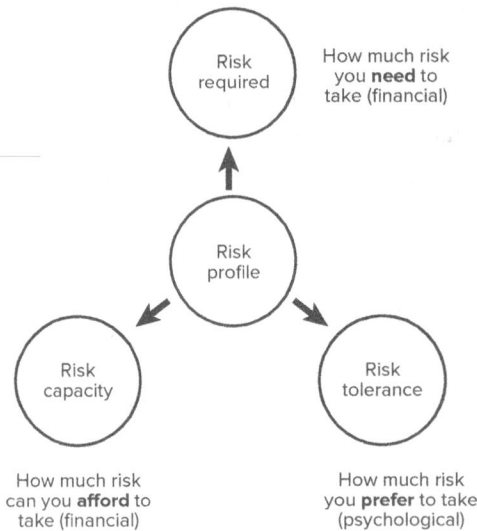

Figure 29: Trinity of investment risk considerations

As we have discussed, these include the extent of your exposure to shares relative to bonds and to the dimensions within those broader asset classes – companies with smaller market capitalisations, lower relative prices and higher profitability within shares, and credit and term risk in bonds.

As you move up the risk spectrum the uncertainty increases, so you need to consider how a major market downturn could derail your plans. If the risk you are contemplating taking is too high, you may need to reconsider your saving and spending rates to ensure your plan is realistic.

The final consideration is how much risk you can tolerate. Let's say your portfolio falls in value by 20 per cent, which is what a portfolio with 60 per cent exposure to growth assets (shares and property) did in the year December 2007 to November 2008. On a $3,000,000 portfolio you are looking at an unrealised loss of $600,000, and in the moment that's pretty confronting.

If you believe there is any risk whatsoever that you will capitulate and sell down the portfolio, then it's not the right portfolio for you. You may well be better off accepting a lower return for less risk but you may also find that you need to trim your expectations on how much you can spend each year from your portfolio.

When considering risk, it can help to visualise your portfolio in terms of buckets of money. There may be a short-term bucket to fund living expenses over the next three to five years, a medium-term bucket to fund liabilities expected in the next five to eight years, and a final bucket containing the riskier return-seeking assets needed to fund longer term liabilities or family legacy.

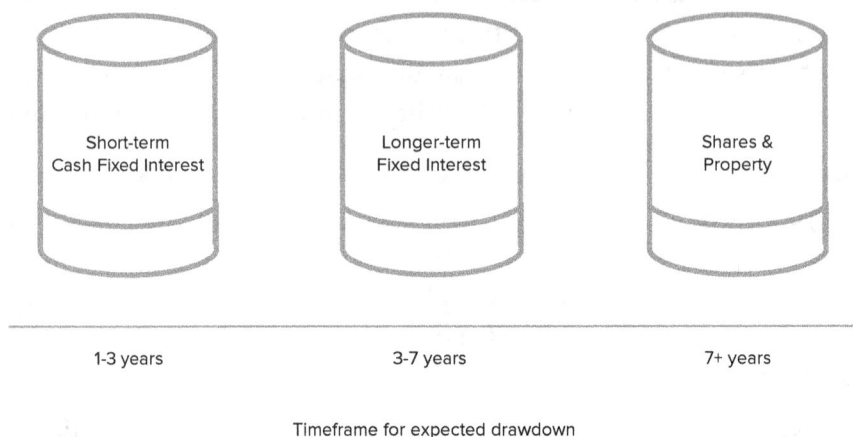

| Short-term Cash Fixed Interest | Longer-term Fixed Interest | Shares & Property |

1-3 years   3-7 years   7+ years

Timeframe for expected drawdown

Figure 30: Buckets of money approach to managing investment risk

While the overall allocation to riskier assets may be 50 per cent or more, knowing that funds are set aside to cover your lifestyle and medium-term liabilities can help you remain disciplined during periods of market volatility.

The asset allocation decision

Having considered how much risk you can and need to take, the next step is to build your asset allocation model. Asset allocation refers to the process of deciding which asset classes you should invest in and in what proportion. Many academic studies show that the majority of the return you will receive will be driven by the mix of assets you choose, rather than your ability to identify better investments or time your way in and out of markets effectively.[31] [32]

Decision 1: Growth and defensive assets – This decision is the biggest driver of your risk and return outcomes. As the names suggest 'growth' assets (shares, property, infrastructure etc), drive the long-

156

term returns in the portfolio while 'defensive' assets (cash and fixed interest) provide a buffer against the inevitable volatility in the share market. In the 11 sample portfolios in Figure 31, Portfolio 1 has 100 per cent in cash. From there, we build each portfolio by decreasing the cash by 10 per cent and adding 10 per cent in shares until we reach Portfolio 11 with a 100 per cent allocation to shares.

We then plot the annualised return from January 1980 to December 2015 against the risk of the portfolio using standard deviation, a measure of portfolio volatility over time. As we can see from Figure 32, there is a neat relationship between increasing return and increasing portfolio risk for each additional 10 per cent allocation of shares we add to the portfolio.

	Cash	Shares	Annualised Return	Annualised Risk (Standard Deviation)
Portfolio 1	100%	0%	8.60%	5.10%
Portfolio 2	90%	10%	9.08%	5.26%
Portfolio 3	80%	20%	9.57%	6.27%
Portfolio 4	70%	30%	10.05%	7.81%
Portfolio 5	60%	40%	10.53%	9.63%
Portfolio 6	50%	50%	11.01%	11.59%
Portfolio 7	40%	60%	11.49%	13.64%
Portfolio 8	30%	70%	11.98%	15.74%
Portfolio 9	20%	80%	12.46%	17.88%
Portfolio 10	10%	90%	12.94%	20.03%
Portfolio 11	0%	100%	13.42%	22.22%

Figure 31: Return and risk characteristics for sample portfolios[33]

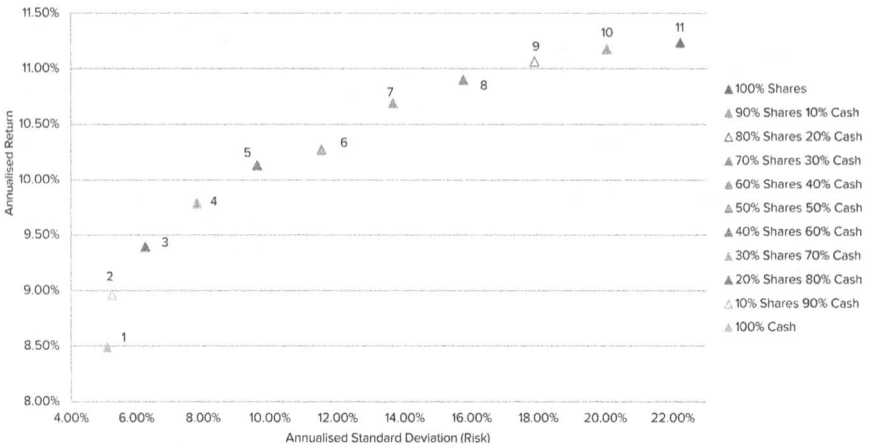

Figure 32: Return-standard deviation chart for sample portfolios[33]

Decision 2: Asset classes and sub-asset classes – There is literally a world of opportunity when it comes to investing in stock and bond markets and other asset classes around the world. Limiting your investment universe to Australia leaves you at risk of missing enormous opportunities in market sectors that Australia offers little exposure to – such as technology, communications, renewable energy, health care and pharmaceuticals, to name a few.

We often see stockbroker portfolios built with up to 90 per cent exposure to Australian shares and with a limited number of shares. This is a crazy approach as the likelihood of the Australian share market being the best performer every year is extremely low and the smaller your portfolio the less likely you are to choose the best stocks in that market.

By building a fully diversified portfolio across more asset and sub-asset classes you are more likely to capture the returns available and minimise the risks of a catastrophic outcome in the event you get a big decision wrong.

This concept of portfolio diversification was introduced in 1952 by US academic Harry Markowitz at the birth of Modern Portfolio Theory. In work that later won him the Nobel Prize in economics,[34] Markowitz found that investors can reduce portfolio risk by holding combinations of assets that are not perfectly correlated. In other words investors can reduce their risk by holding a diversified portfolio of assets.

Major Asset Classes for Australian Investors	
Asset Class	**Sub Asset Classes**
Australian Shares	Australian Large Companies
	Australian Value Companies (Lower Relative Price)
	Australian Smaller Companies
International Shares	International Large Companies
	International Value Companies (Lower Relative Price)
	International Smaller Companies
	Emerging Markets Companies
Fixed Interest	Short-term Fixed Interest
	Medium-term Fixed Interest
	Long-term Fixed Interest
Cash	Cash

Figure 33: Major asset classes for Australian investors

In an ideal world, all investors would enjoy perfect foresight and only invest in the sectors of the market likely to perform best in the period ahead. Unfortunately, the reality is that this is almost impossible. The best approach is to invest in a fully diversified portfolio and to maintain the portfolio allocation in a disciplined way over the long term.

As we see from Figure 34, the returns we receive from markets are random and almost impossible to predict, so by chasing the best performing asset class from year to year we are far more likely to damage our portfolio than add value to it.

	2002	2003	2004	2005	2006	2007	2008	2009	2010	2011	2012	2013	2014	2015
Highest Return	Global Bond 11.57%	Aust Share Small 32.29%	Aust Share Value 31.30%	Emerg Mkt Share 43.20%	Aust Share Small 34.21%	Emerg Mkt Share 25.15%	Global Bond 9.23%	Aust Share Small 57.43%	Aust Share Small 13.05%	Global Bond 10.51%	Aust Share Value 21.64%	Global Share Sml 53.62%	Global Real Est. 32.87%	Global Share Sml 12.13%
	Aust. Cash 4.77%	Global Share Sml 17.92%	Aust Share Large 27.99%	Global Share Sml 23.65%	Global Real Est. 27.90%	Aust Share Small 17.05%	Aust. Cash 7.60%	Aust Share Value 40.86%	Global Share Sml 10.66%	Aust. Cash 5.00%	Aust Share Large 21.00%	Global Share. Lge 47.00%	Global Share. Lge 14.72%	Global Real Est. 11.99%
	Aust Share Value -3.53%	Emerg Mkt Share 16.45%	Global Real Est. 26.84%	Aust Share Large 22.79%	Aust Share Value 24.27%	Aust Share Large 16.12%	Global Share Val -24.92%	Emerg Mkt Share 38.38%	Global Bond 9.28%	Global Real Est. 0.60%	Global Real Est. 20.85%	Global Share Val 46.94%	Global Share Val 13.36%	Global Share. Lge 11.50%
	Global Real Est. -3.67%	Aust Share Large 13.76%	Aust Share Small 26.64%	Aust Share Value 21.67%	Aust Share Large 23.43%	Aust Share Value 10.28%	Global Share. Lge -25.33%	Aust Share Large 36.19%	Global Real Est. 7.11%	Global Share. Lge -5.55%	Emerg Mkt Share 16.74%	Aust Share Value 24.54%	Global Share Sml 11.40%	Aust Share Small 10.16%
	Aust Share Large -8.63%	Aust Share Value 11.20%	Emerg Mkt Share 20.68%	Aust Share Small 19.59%	Emerg Mkt Share 22.98%	Aust. Cash 6.73%	Global Share Sml -26.80%	Global Share Sml 11.73%	Aust. Cash 4.66%	Global Share Val -5.63%	Global Share Sml 16.08%	Aust Share Large 21.54%	Global Bond 10.37%	Global Share Val 7.05%
	Global Small -9.12%	Global Bond 6.59%	Global Share Sml 19.48%	Global Share Val 17.07%	Global Share Val 16.41%	Global Bond 6.63%	Global Real Est. -31.60%	Global Bond 8.03%	Emerg Mkt Share 4.30%	Global Share Sml -9.08%	Global Share. Lge 14.38%	Global Real Est. 18.06%	Aust Share Value 6.97%	Global Bond 3.35%
	Emerg Mkt Share -14.70%	Aust. Cash 4.90%	Global Share Val 13.91%	Global Real 17.00%	Global Share. Lge 11.74%	Global Share. Lge -2.12%	Aust Share Large -37.21%	Aust. Cash 3.47%	Aust Share Value 1.69%	Aust Share Large -9.82%	Global Share Val 14.06%	Emerg Mkt Share 13.03%	Emerg Mkt Share 6.93%	Aust. Cash 2.33%
	Global Share Sml -23.65%	Global Share Val 3.23%	Global Share. Lge 10.26%	Global Share. Lge 16.62%	Global Share Sml 9.07%	Global Share Val -7.18%	Emerg Mkt Share -41.23%	Global Real Est. 2.11%	Aust Share Large 0.83%	Aust Share Value -9.94%	Global Bond 9.66%	Aust. Cash 2.87%	Aust Share Large 6.13%	Aust Share Large 2.14%
	Global Share. Lge -27.17%	Global Real Est. 2.12%	Global Bond 8.92%	Global Bond 6.62%	Aust. Cash 6.02%	Global Share Sml -9.53%	Aust Share Value -41.23%	Global Share. Lge 0.77%	Global Share. Lge -1.94%	Emerg Mkt Share -18.44%	Aust Share Small 6.58%	Global Bond 2.27%	Aust. Cash 2.69%	Aust Share Value 0.51%
Lowest Return	Global Share Val -27.22%	Global Share. Lge -0.52%	Aust. Cash 5.62%	Aust. Cash 5.74%	Global Bond 4.41%	Global Real Est. -20.87%	Aust Share Small -53.17%	Global Share Val -1.80%	Global Share Val -4.35%	Aust Share Small -21.43%	Aust. Cash 3.97%	Aust Share Small -0.76%	Aust Share Small -3.81%	Emerg Mkt Share -4.30%

Figure 34: Randomness of returns in major asset classes [35]

17. Building Your Investment Portfolio

"Success is a science; if you have the conditions, you get the result."

Oscar Wilde

We have now reached the point where we can build a portfolio, employing the benefits of the decades of research and financial theory we have discussed so far. The key concepts used in the construction of these portfolios will enable you to create a portfolio at low cost that adds value above and beyond conventional investment approaches. These concepts are:

- Diversifying your portfolio across different types of assets will reduce risk;

- Combining dissimilar assets can enhance return;

- Diversifying your portfolio internationally broadens your exposures; and,

- Tapping into the dimensions of higher expected return maximises return for a given level of risk.

In building the portfolios we begin with a simple portfolio of cash and internationally diversified shares. From there we gradually add the dimensions of higher expected return. For each portfolio we will be able to see the return we receive and the portfolio volatility (risk) measured by standard deviation.

You will note that with each portfolio we do not alter the split between growth assets (60%) and defensive assets (40%). You might logically expect that as we add components of higher expected return to the portfolio we will increase the overall risk of the portfolio. Let's see what happens.

Portfolio 1

Using the premise that 'a simple portfolio is a good portfolio', our first portfolio is a simple mix of Australian cash and global shares, representing the broadest possible exposure to the global share market we can implement. From January 1980 to December 2015 this portfolio delivered an annualised compound return of 10.23% with an annualised standard deviation of 8.75%, a sound return given the simplicity of the portfolio and the relative ease of implementation and low cost.

Portfolio 1	
Cash	40%
Global Shares	60%

	Annualised Return % (1980-2015)	Annualised Standard Deviation %
Portfolio 1	10.23%	8.75%

Portfolio 2

Now we split our allocation of shares between global and Australian shares. As we can see, this small shift increases our annualised return to 10.59% and decreases our risk score to 8.11% per annum, reflecting the diversification benefit we receive from being fully diversified in a share portfolio.

Portfolio 2

Cash	40%
Global Shares	30%
Australian Shares	30%

	Annualised Return % (1980-2015)	Annualised Standard Deviation %
Portfolio 1	10.23%	8.75%
Portfolio 2	10.59%	8.11%

Portfolio 3

Now we begin to introduce the dimensions we would expect to deliver a higher return. First we substitute our 40% defensive component from cash into diversified short-term fixed interest. While the latter has a higher expected return than cash, our exposure is limited to the most highly rated government, semi-government and corporate bonds.

We then substitute our exposure to the broad market indexes to introduce the *Profitability* dimension by investing in funds with profitable large company exposure. From there, we introduce the *Value* (relative price) dimension of return to our portfolio.

Again, we see that our annualised return increases and our risk decreases. This result is somewhat counter-intuitive because with the addition of the *Value* dimension we might expect our portfolio risk to increase, not decrease. This is the real benefit of diversification, where we can add assets of differing risk levels to a portfolio and the interplay between them decreases our overall portfolio volatility without reducing return.

Portfolio 3

Short Term Fixed Interest	40%
Global Large Companies	15%
Australian Large Companies	15%
Global Value Companies	15%
Australian Value Companies	15%

	Annualized Return % (1980-2015)	Annualized Standard Deviation %
Portfolio 1	10.23%	8.75%
Portfolio 2	10.59%	8.11%
Portfolio 3	11.20%	7.97%

Portfolio 4

Our final portfolio introduces the smaller company dimension, by splitting the allocation we had made to value shares equally between smaller company and value shares across both global and Australian shares. We now have our share market components spread across large, value and small companies, and diversified across Australian and global shares. Each component is then tilted in favour of more profitable companies.

Again we see a marked increase in return over the investment period with only a very slight increase in portfolio volatility.

Portfolio 4	
Short Term Fixed Interest	40%
Global Large Companies	15%
Australian Large Companies	15%
Global Value Companies	7.5%
Australian Value Companies	7.5%
Global Small Companies	7.5%
Australian Small Companies	7.5%

	Annualised Return % (1980-2015)	Annualised Standard Deviation %
Portfolio 1	10.23%	8.75%
Portfolio 2	10.59%	8.11%
Portfolio 3	11.20%	7.97%
Portfolio 4	11.59%	8.04%

Summary

In an ideal world, we would eliminate investment risk completely. While we can't do that, we can mitigate risk by using these dimensions of return. This approach enables investors to use an evidence-based approach rather than employing the more conventional approaches of stock picking, guru following and speculating more generally.

While no one can guarantee what future returns will be, this approach enables investors to effectively and efficiently capture the benefits markets have to offer in an evidence-based and low-cost way. This last point is very important, as every dollar of investment cost saved is an additional dollar available to fund your long-term goals.

While there are many other investment strategies available, such as hedge funds, long/short funds, private equity, gold, commodities, water trading and initial public offers (IPOs), they all require a degree of speculation and uncertainty. These structures also tend to be far higher in cost than the asset class approach, so while the prospect of high rewards is alluring, careful consideration needs to be given to where these alternative investment approaches fit in your overall strategy.

The valuation-based approach described above is reliable, transparent and maximises the expected return for each given level of risk. The sample portfolios in Figure 35 provide a great guide for you to consider your risk and return objectives and to place into perspective the trade-offs you will need to consider as an investor.

RISKY ASSET #1

RISKY ASSET #2

A PORTFOLIO
OF BOTH

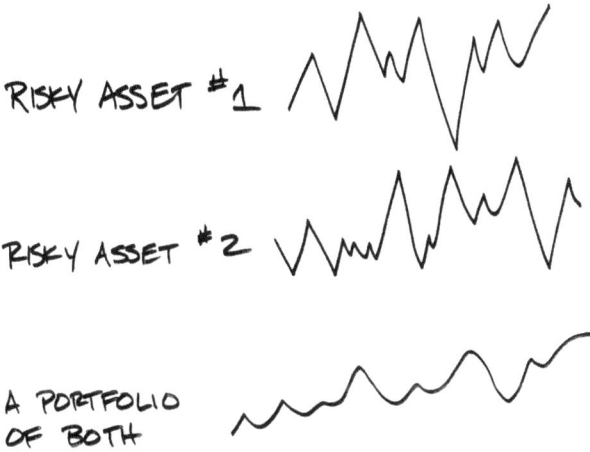

Validation Portfolios

	Portfolio A	Portfolio B	Portfolio C	Portfolio D	Portfolio E	Portfolio F
GROWTH EXPOSURE	0%	20%	40%	60%	80%	100%
DEFENSIVE EXPOSURE	100%	80%	60%	40%	20%	0%
Australian Shares	0%	8%	16%	24%	32%	40%
- Australia Large Companies Index	0%	4%	8%	12%	16%	20%
- Australia Value Companies Index	0%	2%	5%	7%	10%	12%
- Australia Small Companies Index	0%	2%	3%	5%	5%	8%
Global Shares	0%	8%	16%	24%	32%	40%
- Global Large Companies Index	0%	4%	8%	12%	16%	20%
- Global Value Companies Index	0%	2%	5%	7%	10%	12%
- Global Small Companies Index	0%	2%	3%	5%	5%	8%
Emerging Markets Shares	0%	3%	6%	9%	12%	15%
- Emerging Markets Value Index	0%	3%	6%	9%	12%	15%
Property	0%	1%	2%	3%	4%	5%
- S&P/ASX A-REIT Index	0%	1%	2%	3%	4%	5%
Fixed Interest	100%	80%	60%	40%	20%	0%
- Bloomberg AusBond Bank Bill Index	100%	80%	60%	40%	20%	0%
ONE-YEAR TOTAL RETURN (%)	2.3	2.9	3.3	3.8	4.0	4.4
THREE-YEAR ANNUALISED RETURN (%)	2.6	4.9	7.2	9.5	11.8	14.2
FIVE-YEAR ANNUALISED RETURN (%)	3.4	4.6	5.8	7.0	8.2	9.4
TEN-YEAR ANNUALISED RETURN (%)	4.5	4.9	5.3	5.6	5.8	6.0
FIFTEEN-YEAR ANNUALISED RETURN (%)	4.8	5.5	6.1	6.8	7.3	7.8
TWENTY-YEAR ANNUALISED RETURN (%)	5.1	6.1	7.1	8.0	8.9	9.7
ANNUALISED RETURN (1990-2015)	5.9	6.8	7.7	8.6	9.4	10.1
ANNUALISED STANDARD DEV. (1990-2015)	0.8	2.4	4.7	7.0	9.4	11.7
LOWEST ONE YEAR RETURN (%)	2.3 (01/15-12/15)	-2.4 (01/08-12/08)	-11.4 (01/08-12/08)	-20.0 (01/08-12/08)	-27.8 (01/08-12/08)	-35.0 (01/08-12/08)
LOWEST ANNUALISED THREE-YEAR RETURN (%)	2.6 (01/13-12/15)	3.1 (09/07-08/10)	-0.1 (04/06-03/09)	-3.4 (04/06-03/09)	-6.7 (04/06-03/09)	-10.0 (04/06-03/09)
HIGHEST ONE YEAR RETURN (%)	16.1 (01/90-12/90)	14.7 (01/91-12/91)	22.9 (02/93-01/94)	32.6 (02/93-01/94)	42.9 (02/93-01/94)	54.0 (02/93-01/94)
HIGHEST ANNUALISED THREE-YEAR RETURN (%)	11.4 (01/90-12/90)	11.7 (10/90-09/93)	15.2 (02/91-01/94)	19.2 (02/91-01/94)	23.7 (04/03-03/06)	28.7 (04/03-03/06)
NEGATIVE QUARTERS (1990-2015)	0	12	18	25	28	28
GROWTH OF $1	$4.44	$5.59	$6.96	$8.50	$10.27	$12.18

Figure 35: Validation portfolios for asset class investors[36]

18. Investor Discipline

"What lies in our power to do, lies in our power not to do."

Aristotle

Having carefully constructed your portfolio around these evidence-based principles, specifically to complement your strategic plan, you will want to make sure it is properly maintained. This is where you may well end up fighting against human nature to achieve the best possible investment outcome.

A whole branch of science called behavioural finance has evolved to study the interaction between human behaviour and economics. One of its pioneers, Daniel Kahneman, received the 2002 Nobel Prize in Economic Sciences in recognition of his work.

What Kahneman and others have learned is that as humans we are essentially 'hard wired' to act in ways that are not necessarily in our financial best interest. Instead, we respond irrationally, mainly guided by fear and greed. Many investors grossly miss the returns available to them due to poor investment behaviour. This behaviour appears in many forms, but four traits – overconfidence, risk aversion, recency and regret – are especially significant. When we examine these traits closely it is easy to see how successful and intelligent people can find themselves susceptible to them.

Back in caveman times we humans evolved with a very strong sense of self-preservation. Any hint of 'rustling in the grass' was interpreted as a potential threat and our *fight or flight* response kicked in, either to defend ourselves or to seek safety.

This fight-flight response is something we can all relate to – recall the adrenalin rush after a 'near miss' or the gut-wrenching feeling of fear we experienced from a perceived threat. This feeling is an automatic response to negative stimuli created by the amygdala, which resides deep in our brain.

Understanding the autonomic response really matters when it comes to a discussion on the emotions around financial markets. When markets go through periods of extreme volatility many of us have a deep-rooted response in our amygdala, generating a deeply uncomfortable feeling of fear. The fear created is automatic – we can't control it – and it often deeply motivates us to do something. This can involve selling down a portfolio at the worst possible time, with awful consequences, before markets inevitably recover and rise again.

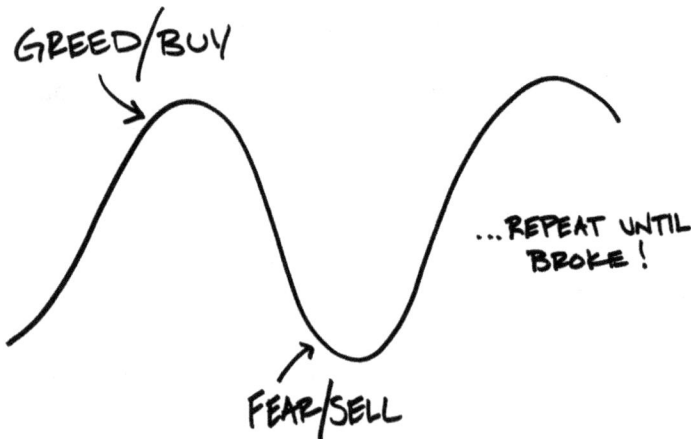

GREED/BUY

...REPEAT UNTIL BROKE!

FEAR/SELL

Research organisation Dalbar Inc found that in the 20 years to December 2014, the return of the S&P 500 Index was 9.85 per cent while the average US investor in managed funds received 5.19 per cent, an underperformance margin of 3.66 percentage points. [37] While fees, tax and other factors explain some of the difference, the largest single contributor was the average investor being unwilling to stay firmly invested right through and out the other side of a market downturn.

While long-term investing can be challenging, Figure 36 clearly shows that 'market timing' is risky. The annual compound return from April 2000 to December 2015, a period that included the GFC, was 8 per cent. But an investor who was out of the market on the best trading days missed out on the considerable recovery that occurred after the initial market downturn.

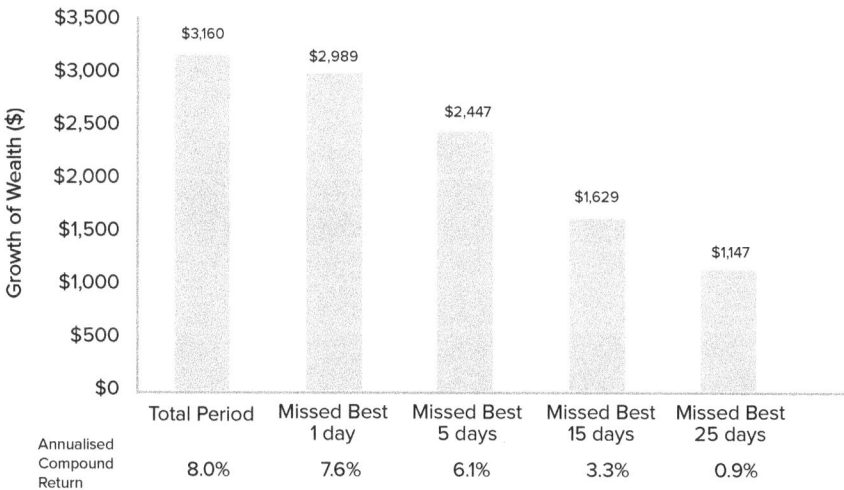

	Total Period	Missed Best 1 day	Missed Best 5 days	Missed Best 15 days	Missed Best 25 days
Growth of Wealth ($)	$3,160	$2,989	$2,447	$1,629	$1,147
Annualised Compound Return	8.0%	7.6%	6.1%	3.3%	0.9%

Figure 36: market timing risk S&P/ASX 200 index[38]

173

Financial markets will always be volatile, and the best way to manage your emotions is through education and information. By understanding our own emotions we can better deal with the inevitable ups and downs we will experience.

Overconfidence

Overconfidence is the tendency of human beings to think we're smarter or more capable than we really are. Many intelligent people assume that because they're good at what they do, they will also excel at managing their investments. This tendency reveals itself in the practice of market timing, trading shares and speculating in small opportunistic shares. Speculating in an attempt to outperform the market as a whole is a challenge. Numerous studies have shown that efforts to beat the market actually have the opposite effect over the long term, and yet many people have a strong gambler instinct that they find hard to overcome.

The call from a stockbroker with an opportunity to invest in the next 'hot' IPO often results in investors parting with their hard-earned cash. Similarly, when a favourite share is going up it is common to feel that it will keep going. No one wants to be the one leaving the party early. This is evident when a particular market sector is booming. Whether it is gold, iron ore or biotechnology, there will always be a sector that is 'hot'. You need to balance your fear of missing out against the possibility that you'll be left holding your shares at big losses after everyone else has left the party.

Risk aversion

Another behavioural weakness in finance is risk aversion— which might better be described as loss aversion, since it occurs even when risk is not a factor. Academic research has found that investors are more troubled by loss than they are excited by an equivalent gain. It stands to reason, then, that an investor seeking to minimise loss may reduce the opportunity for gain.

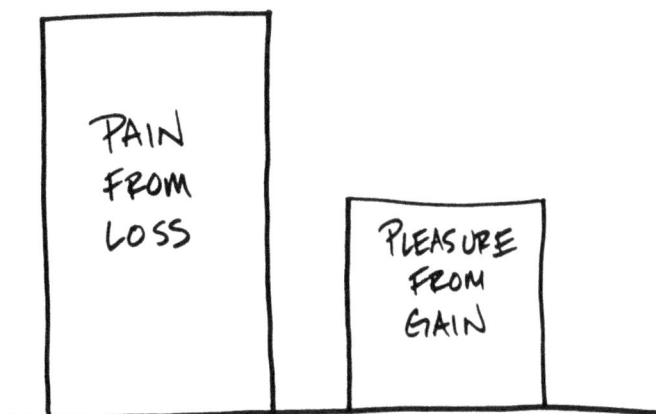

In their research Kahneman and Tversky[39] found that the pain of loss in giving up $50 is almost double that of the pleasure of gaining $50. This is valuable knowledge when we consider the discomfort a falling share market can create.

Translated, their findings suggest that when our portfolio gains $20,000 the happiness we experience is half the sense of *unhappiness* we experience when the portfolio falls by a similar amount. This explains the extreme feeling of discomfort we can have when markets drop significantly and media headlines scream of doom.

In the face of loss aversion, the best strategy is to keep your head and stay the course, knowing that your portfolio structure, a diversified approach and time are your best allies.

Recency

As humans, we regularly use our past experiences to try to predict the future. But it doesn't help much with investments. Investors often look at short-term events—a run-up of technology shares, for instance – as an indication of a money-making trend. The mentality is something like this: If the market (or a particular hot stock) is going up, up, up, we don't want to miss out.

Investment companies, stockbrokers and fund managers are good at understanding and exploiting this human weakness. No sooner has a sector taken off than special research reports and products will begin to appear on the market. It's no surprise that the marketing wrapped around these products is designed to appeal to our fear of missing out. After all, if recent past performance is irrelevant, why is it touted so heavily in advertising? The only problem is, by the time we've heard about it, the moment to invest may have passed.

Regret

Another human trait that impacts on investing is that we are very quick to judge ourselves if the outcome of our decision-making isn't immediately positive.

Investing can be a big decision and as the size and importance of the portfolio increases, the emotional responses can potentially become more acute. As an investor, you don't want to find yourself in a position where you are led by regret to sell an investment after a market decline, even though you made the investment for the long term and as part of an asset allocation strategy.

Equally, some researchers feel that fear of regret can lead to bad decisions: like holding on to a loser too long for fear of owning up to having purchased it in the first place.

To these four, I would add two additional behavioural traits common to investors in today's society.

Competitiveness

This factor has numerous effects. In a way it is the keeping up with the Joneses syndrome again in a different guise. Humans are naturally competitive and we don't like missing out on a deal or an opportunity, particularly when there is a degree of social status associated with being involved. This is compounded by the fact we like to see ourselves as at least as successful, if not more successful, than our colleagues and peers.

The private banking arms of all banks trade off this human weakness. By making their offerings more 'exclusive' they appeal to people's egos and the desire not to miss out. Products like hedge funds are also marketed this way. Almost all VIP offers should be closely examined as they tend to be simple ideas wrapped inside exclusive packaging with high profit margins.

Competitiveness can lead investors to seek the highest possible return on their investments, regardless of their real goals, and to look for speculative winners. Most successful investment strategies should be quite simple. In most cases, the more complex or exclusive an offering, the warier you should be.

Time constraint

Lastly, life seems to be getting busier and busier for all of us. Lack of time is often cited as a reason for not taking control of our investments and just letting things drift. When we arrive home on a Friday evening after a long week of work, the last thing many of us feel like doing is sitting down to research our investment strategies.

When our financial well-being is so closely tied to the way we save and invest, finding a simple and reliable way to invest makes so much sense.

19. Maintaining Your Portfolio

"There's no such thing as a free lunch."

Milton Friedman

Having established a portfolio of high quality, long term investments there will be some housekeeping required from time to time.

Rebalancing

Warren Buffet likes to say that the key to investment success is to "be greedy when everyone else is fearful and fearful when everyone else is greedy". However, we have discussed in some detail the difficulty associated with timing markets. So how *do* we best maintain our portfolio?

The best way to maintain your portfolio is to rebalance regularly. In a diversified investment portfolio that is never rebalanced, (i.e. buy-and-hold), the benefits of diversification are eroded over time as higher-returning asset classes gradually earn themselves higher portfolio weighting, and lower-returning asset classes gradually end up with lower portfolio weights. This can lead to portfolio risk-return characteristics getting out of balance. In the case of shares, an extended period of market growth can result in your portfolio becoming over-exposed, thus lifting the overall risk of your portfolio to a level you never intended. As we have previously acknowledged, we can't remove risk completely but you can maintain your preferred risk exposures.

...SELL A LITTLE

X

...BUY A BIT

Y

[RE-BALANCE]

Systematic rebalancing enforces the discipline of selling assets when they have gone up in value and buying assets when they are down in price. This may seem counter-intuitive – it is tempting to hold on to assets that have done well (your favourites) and you may be reluctant to buy more of the assets that have performed poorly (the dogs).

Buying low and selling high is precisely the discipline we want to employ, yet it is exactly the opposite of what many investors do. Remember that no asset class remains the best performer forever so a disciplined approach to rebalancing can help you manage your risk and your wealth preservation.

While this all seems very simple, in practice it is a little more complex. We need to be mindful of taxes and portfolio liquidity, particularly for those investors who are drawing down on pension portfolios. While the research on portfolio rebalancing does not point to an optimal time interval for rebalancing it makes sense to rebalance at least annually, or when the situation arises for an 'opportunistic' rebalance.

Creating portfolio triggers for your rebalancing strategy will help guide the decision. For example, you may consider rebalancing your share market exposure if it increases by more than 10 per cent. So if you intend your share market exposure to be 40 per cent and through market growth it has increased to 44 percent, a rebalance would bring the share market portfolio weight back to the intended 40 per cent. Bear in mind that transaction costs and taxes could undermine the benefit of the rebalance if the numbers involved are too small so care needs to be taken to ensure the rebalance is adding value to the portfolio.

Minimise costs

In most areas of life the adage, *you get what you pay for* plays out, but this is certainly not an assumption you can rely on when you invest. Investment management costs can have a major impact on your portfolio and therefore your outcome, and while the average fee paid by investors in Australia is relatively competitive by world standards, it doesn't mean you shouldn't care about the costs you pay. While cheap doesn't necessarily equal best, there is a strong case for being aware of your investment costs and keeping them as low as possible.

Earlier, I outlined how few of the active fund managers outperform their index on an after-fees basis. I find it interesting that so many investors habitually overpay for a service that simply isn't delivered consistently. Can you imagine continuing to pay for daily newspaper delivery if the paper arrived only occasionally? Of course not. And yet Australian investors do this routinely.

The average fee in Australia for an actively managed wholesale share fund was at the time of writing 1.02% per annum, and for bond funds 0.56% per annum.[40] In addition, funds that trade regularly will incur costs in the form of broker commissions and bid-ask spreads. These additional costs are opaque but detract from investor returns. While wholesale funds offer somewhat lower prices, retail funds are significantly more expensive, with fees ranging well over the 2 per cent mark.

Fund Type	Low Fee	High Fee	Comments
Hedge Funds	1.75%	3.5%	Performance fees may apply
Acitvely Managed Funds (wholesale)	0.65%	1.45%	Performance fees may apply
Actively Managed Funds (retail)	1.25%	2.45%	Performance fees may apply
Index Funds	0.10%	0.50%	n/a
Asset Class Funds	0.20%	0.70%	n/a

Figure 37: Indicative investment costs[41]

While fees should never be your only focus it does make sense to ensure you are getting value for money and getting what you pay for. The investment strategy outlined in this section is not the only way to invest, but it's a very reliable way to capture the returns you need to fund your goals.

Section Take-outs

....

....

....

....

....

....

....

....

....

....

PART IV

LEGACY PLANNING

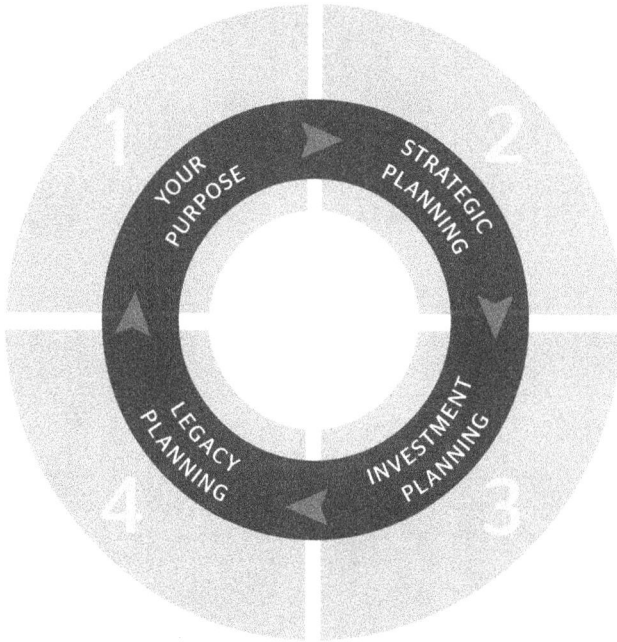

20. What is a Legacy?

"I would hope my legacy would be bringing smiles to faces."

Janet Jackson

It would be easy to define legacy just in terms of your Will but there's far more to it than that. Your *Legacy Plan* represents who you are, your place in the world, the contribution you make to others and how you will be remembered by those you care about.

Legacy planning is often the highest planning priority for a large part of the population we describe as *Family Stewards*. These are the people for whom family is their single highest priority in life, and they want to ensure their wealth is used to care for their family during their lifetime and beyond. They will also place a high priority on protecting their family's long term interests.

Careful legacy planning ensures every contingency is thought through, so that no matter what happens in your life there is a plan to protect you, your family and your wealth. And far from being relevant just for a few very wealthy families, a legacy plan is relevant for all families, creating security and passing on important family values to future generations.

From time to time we see situations where the unexpected death of a parent leaves the remaining family in a perilous financial state because a lack of planning has left the family without the resources it needs to carry on with their lifestyle. We also see situations where after the death of the last surviving parent, a bitter feud ensues with one family member pitting themselves against others to gain their 'rightful' share of the assets.

We believe these situations can be avoided through careful planning and open communication among family members. No one likes discussion about death and dying, but like so many conversations we need to have with the people we care about, conversations about legacy can be fulfilling and can set your family up for success beyond your lifetime.

Legacy planning begins with an assessment of the human risks your family faces and therefore your *Insurance Plan*. The disablement or premature death of the primary income earner will mean the family no longer has the benefit of their income. Overnight, a family that was once financially secure is suddenly pondering their future. A well prepared insurance plan will cover gaps in a family's financial position and will ensure financial security in the event of the unexpected.

In family businesses, appropriate risk assessment can mean the difference between the survival or failure of the enterprise if a key person dies. Proper insurance planning can provide the funding needed to ensure the continuation of a business after the death of an important contributor.

Next comes your *Estate Plan*, which deals with the distribution of your assets and passes control of trusts, superannuation and companies in an orderly manner. For wealthier families, much of your wealth may not be held in your own name, and when a family business or farm is involved careful thought will be required to ensure a smooth and harmonious transition.

An estate plan is comprised of the legal documents, Wills and enduring powers of guardianship and attorney, and the important conversations that explain the decisions and expectations contained in the Will.

Last we deal with your *Giving Plan*, which deals with the contribution you make to your family, the community and charitable pursuits. Giving may not include money, but may be expressed through the giving of your time and skills to the causes you care about.

We all want to be remembered for happy memories and the contribution we make to the lives of our family and others, and not for any financial mess we may leave behind. The time we spend on our legacy plan will ensure that every contingency is carefully considered and where appropriate a solution can be put in place.

21. Managing Life's Risks

"Family is the first essential cell of human society."

Pope John XXIII

A key aspect of legacy planning is taking the time to consider the risks you face. Many risks can be managed by purchasing insurance and your need for insurance will depend on your financial resources and commitments. Where your asset position is considerably greater than your lifetime spending requirements, you will have little need for life insurance, however like most people, you may choose to insure your physical assets like homes, commercial property, boats, cars and so on.

As you consider the use of insurance as part of your financial plan we need to remember that the sole purpose of insurance is to replace an economic loss, so as you work through this chapter it is important to identify *if a risk exists* and if it does, to *quantify your exposure*. Once the exposure is understood, it is easy to create a solution using insurance that balances the impact of the risk on your family's position against the cost of eliminating the risk.

Here we categorise the risks we face into three areas:

a. protection for human risks.

b. protection for physical assets and general risks.

c. protection for legal risks.

Human assets

The loss or long term illness of a key financial contributor can place the achievement of your family's goals in jeopardy, and put family business interests at risk. As the primary income earner in my family, I have always been acutely aware of the financial difficulty my family would face if I died or could not work for an extended period of time. By having a contingency plan for the worst outcomes, you can have peace of mind that no matter what hand you are dealt in life, your family and business interests are well protected.

While insurance will never take away the pain of loss of a loved one or remove the anguish of a serious long term illness, it can resolve much of the financial stress.

Personal insurance is used to fill financial gaps created on the death or illness of an individual. For example, a young professional couple may be paying off a sizeable mortgage at the same time as they are raising a young family and making plans for a private school education. If the key income earner dies or is incapacitated the family's capability to pay the mortgage and the school fees is in doubt, as is the family's long term income.

Protecting your wealth and your standard of living is as important as building it - by clearly understanding the risks you face, you can create a plan relevant to you and your family. While there are many online insurance services available, this is an area where the right advice can be extremely valuable, as too little insurance leaves gaps in your family's security, while being over-insured wastes money that should be channeled into funding your goals. The types of insurances you may consider are outlined below.

Life Insurance - Provides a lump sum payment in the event of death or a terminal illness. When determining your need for life insurance, you will need to consider your family's ongoing income requirements, debt commitments and education requirements as a start.

Total and Permanent Disablement - Provides a lump sum payment should you suffer an illness or injury which totally and permanently prevents you from working again. It can assist with medical/ rehabilitation costs and provide a level of financial security if you are never able to work again.

Health Events and Trauma - Provides a lump sum benefit in the event that you suffer a "critical condition" as defined by the insurance provider. It covers events such as a heart attack, stroke, cancer, brain tumors and many other traumatic health conditions. This type of cover is designed to help you recover financially during a period of prolonged medical recovery, to pay for expensive medical treatments, childcare and to help the family to operate as normally as possible during a period of significant disruption and distress.

Income Protection - Provides a regular benefit in the form of a monthly income if you are unable to work due to sickness or injury. Income protection benefits are only paid after an agreed waiting period that may range from 30 days up to two years and the amount paid is normally set at no more that 85% of the income you received prior to your illness or injury. Depending on the length of the illness the monthly payments may continue until you are fully recovered and back at work, or may continue until the agreed benefit end date which may be as late as your 70th birthday.

How much cover will I need?

Assessing the cover you need will be important to ensure a balance is found between covering the need, and not paying more premiums than is absolutely necessary. To establish how much life insurance cover is needed you will need to establish the difference between your current available investment assets and the capital required to fund your needs and goals if the primary income earner was unable to work.

Figure 38: The insurance needs equation

Take the example of a financially established family whose lifestyle is dependent on the highest earning parent's professional income. Let's say that all of their financial plans are on track. They are paying down their debt on schedule, they are saving regularly towards retirement and their children's private school expenses are met comfortably from their household cash flow.

All other things being equal, we would conclude that the family is headed for financial security, except that is, if the highest income earner dies or is unable to work for a long period. All of a sudden a very healthy financial picture faces considerable stress and disruption.

There is no right answer to exactly how much insurance is needed however it would make sense in this scenario to ensure the family has adequate insurance funding to cover living expenses, education and debt repayment at a minimum. The table below outlines the calculation that may be appropriate for the family.

Needs in the Event of Primary Income Earner's Death	
Surviving spouse's earnings	$75,000
Additional living expenses needed	$60,000
Years required	40
Capital required to fund future income	*$1,400,000*
Mortgage payout	$700,000
Education funding	$320,000
Funeral and other expenses	$25,000
Total future funding required	*$2,445,000*
Less current investment capital	$420,000
Total life insurance required	*$2,025,000*

Figure 39: Sample life insurance calculation

A sound planning principle is to reduce insurance cover progressively as the family's wealth position increases over time. As we get older the statistical risk of death and disablement increases, so insurance companies will charge considerably more to insure a 50-year-old compared with someone in their thirties. Achieving a level of financial security by your mid-50's enables you to reduce the level of your insurance freeing up funds towards your investment plans.

Rice Warner actuaries estimate that the minimum life insurance needed for Australian couples in their mid-thirties is 10 times their combined annual earnings. In my experience the right number is probably closer to 20 times annual earnings. This is an area that parents with adult children should also be aware of, particularly if there is any possibility that in the event of a catastrophic life event for the adult child, the parents may feel obliged to assist their children financially. Encouraging your adult children to be adequately insured will provide protection for your retirement plans too.

Business risk insurance

Human capital is the most valuable asset many small and medium businesses have, and yet the focus normally turns to the protection of physical assets; buildings, equipment, vehicles and so on. Business thrives as a result of the hard work and ingenuity of the owners and employees, yet we rarely place sufficient value on the important human capital we have within the business.

If you are a business owner, consider for a moment how your business would cope with lack of leadership, operational disruption and reduced earnings if one of the key people could no longer work? How would the business deal with nervous creditors? If a key person died, could the ownership of the business be transferred in an orderly way to continuing business partners?

When considering the human risks we face in business there are three areas we need to be aware of.

Key person – when one or more people are considered *key people* in small or medium enterprise, their contribution is such that the business would struggle to survive without their ongoing input. To provide greater certainty for the business key person insurance provides a lump sum benefit on the death or permanent disablement of a key person. While the funds can never fully replace the key person, they will provide the business with breathing space to deal with any downturn in operating revenue and the costs associated with recruiting replacement personnel.

Succession – a sound succession plan enables the smooth exit of a business partner in the event of death or total disablement. A legal agreement between the business owners, known as a shareholder or succession agreement, needs to be in place to ensure an orderly transfer of ownership from the deceased's family to continuing owners. Ideally, the agreement would spell out the terms and conditions of the transfer and would provide a method to value the business.

Where the business has grown significantly in value, it can be very difficult for the continuing shareholders to fund the purchase price to ensure the transaction can take place. This situation can create significant difficulties as the continuing business owners need control over future decisions while the family of the deceased is entitled to a say in the business for so long as they continue as owners.

An insurance policy that is specifically put in place to fund a succession event can provide certainty for both the continuing owners and the deceased's family.

Debt protection – many small and medium businesses fund their business growth through borrowings primarily through their banks.

Where debt facilities are considerable, the owners will almost always provide personal guarantees over their own assets to ensure that if the business goes bad, the bank has recourse to the business owner's personal assets to ensure repayment is made.

In a situation where the death or disablement of a business owner causes the business to falter, a nervous lender will place their own shareholders' interests ahead of the business owner's, and any shortfall in the repayment of the debt will be pursued to the business owner's estate. In these circumstances, an insurance policy to cover the debt exposure to the bank provides certainty that in the event of the death of the guarantor, the bank's exposure can be settled.

Policy ownership

The way you structure the ownership of your insurances will have a significant impact on the cost of the insurance and the tax treatment of any payouts. For example, you might weigh up the benefits of obtaining insurance through a superannuation fund rather than buying it personally with your after-tax funds.

This area requires careful consideration, and you may benefit from appropriate planning advice. A life insurance specialist will be very valuable in helping you structure your affairs appropriately.

Physical and general risks

Many people would consider it strange to consider property and other forms of general insurance as part of the broader wealth management plan, however a catastrophic event like the loss of a home to a fire can put a significant dent in a family's financial plan.

I don't claim any professional expertise in this area although there have been a number of real events where we have identified risks which our clients would have otherwise have been unaware.

In one case, a client of ours had built a home in one of Perth's blue ribbon suburbs and had duly insured the property for its replacement value. Some twenty years later we were diligently working through our checklist of risk issues our client might face, only to find that the policy had been renewed but not reviewed in the 20 years since it had been taken out. As our client was a busy surgeon it was understandable how this could happen, but a building insured for $320,000 some 20 years earlier was now worth a seven-figure sum. In the event of a fire and total loss, the underinsurance would have placed a large hole in their financial plan.

While our insurance renewals come and go, it pays to occasionally check cover levels to ensure they are adequate, and if you are unsure check with a general insurance specialist.

Legal risks

Many professions and occupations have associated legal risks that must be managed to protect your personal financial interests. Lawyers, dentists, surgeons, consulting engineers and many other professionals are exposed to potentially high risk decisions that in rare circumstances, place them in a position where they are subjected to legal proceedings and claim. Similarly, anyone who signs up to be a company director is potentially exposing their personal assets to claim.

The only antidote to manage these potential risks is to ensure your asset ownership is arranged so that important assets like the family home are not unnecessarily exposed to risk, and to ensure your professional risks insurance policies are adequate and up to date. Insurances such as medical indemnity, professional indemnity and directors and officer's liability (D&O) are all designed to protect the individual in circumstances where well-intentioned actions result in less than ideal outcomes.

A specialist general insurance broker is the best person to advise on the insurance aspects of legal risk protection while a financial adviser or accountant in concert with an asset protection lawyer can assist with establishing your business structures to achieve maximum protection.

Now let's take a look at estate planning.

RISK

EXPOSURE

22. Creating an Estate Plan

"In this world nothing can be said to be certain, except death and taxes."

Benjamin Franklin

Having a well considered estate plan is the first step in helping your family deal with your affairs after your death. It is sad when there is conflict over the distribution of an estate, a situation that can be avoided with better planning and clear communication so if a harmonious outcome is what you are seeking, this chapter will help.

Your estate plan should provide your family with a clear roadmap of what needs to be done to distribute the estate in line with your wishes and to protect the assets for the benefit of family members. An estate plan will also deal with your personal affairs during your lifetime if you are unable to deal with them personally.

Creating a will

No one over the age of 18 should die without a will and yet it is estimated that over half of the adult population in Australia doesn't have one. Even a simple will is better than nothing as it will avoid having your assets distributed in line with a set formula prescribed by the state of Australia you live in. Known as intestacy, dying without a will can create tension and complexity in families that is best avoided.

Your will is a document best prepared by a specialist estate planning lawyer, as a declaration of your personal wishes regarding your estate and appoints an executor to distribute your property. The executor of your estate is the person you appoint to administer your estate from the date of death to the point where the assets are distributed to the beneficiaries.

Responsibilities of the executor

Your executor needs to be a person or people you trust implicitly to do the right thing, and to administer the estate efficiently and effectively. In the event of death, the executor has many responsibilities including:

- Locating the will and notify the beneficiaries;

- Ensuring that the beneficiaries are not suffering unnecessary financial difficulties due to the sudden change of circumstances;

- To safeguard the estate by identifying and valuing all assets and liabilities and ensuring the assets are appropriately insured and protected;

- Applying to the Supreme Court to obtain probate of the will, which gives the executor the authority to administer the deceased's estate; and,

- Taking care of any financial issues such as completing tax returns and paying all debts including funeral expenses, estate administration fees and any creditors.

The executor may be your spouse, a family member, a trusted friend or one or more of your professional advisers like your lawyer, financial adviser or accountant.

Role of the trustee

Once the executor has wound up the estate, the assets will be available to be distributed to the beneficiaries. However, there are many

testamentary trust is taxed at normal adult tax rates. If a trustee of a testamentary trust distributes income to several child beneficiaries, each of them is entitled to the full tax free threshold, currently $20,542 per annum.

Testamentary trust case study

Michael and Sarah have a thorough estate plan in place and Michael dies before Sarah. Michael has nominated his estate as the beneficiary of his superannuation and life insurance so all of his assets form part of his estate.

Sarah requests the executor of Michael's estate to do the best thing for her and their three children and so she needs to consider the options. Sarah continues to earn income of $60,000 per annum from other work. The first consideration has Sarah inheriting all the assets personally and not using a testamentary trust. As Sarah is the only taxpayer the income cannot be spread between her and her children.

Source of Income	Sarah
Income	$60,000
Inherited income (earning 4% pa)	$70,000
Total income	$130,000
Tax	$38,647
After tax income	$91,353

Figure 40: Income and tax without testamentary trust

Next, the executor considers establishing a testamentary trust using $1,750,000 of assets from Michael's estate. By using the testamentary trust, the trustee can spread the distribution of income across Sarah and her three children. As a result of using a testamentary trust, Sarah's tax liability falls from $38,647 to $14,469; an annual tax saving of $24,178. This tax saving may be even higher to the extent that the trust derives fully franked dividends.

Source of Income	Sarah	Trust
Income	$60,000	
Inherited income (earning 4% pa)		$70,000
Total income	$60,000	$70,000
Tax	$12,147	$2,322
After tax income	$48,853	$67,678

Figure 41: Income and tax with a testamentary trust

This outcome is possible because the income of the trust has been applied for the benefit of her children to pay for their care and education and so it will be taxed at their low marginal tax rates. The trustee will be responsible for paying this tax on the children's behalf.

These same tax benefits are available when an inheritance passes from a parent to their adult children and grandchildren. The creation of a legacy through a testamentary trust can assist future generations by protecting family wealth in trust structures that offer greater legal protection from family breakdown and legal claim, as well as considerable tax advantages.

Executor → Will

Appointor & Trustee ⇢ Discretionary Testamentary Trust ← Benefits:
- Flexible distributions
- Asset protection
- Tax savings (especially for minor beneficiaries)

May be the primary beneficiary and/or an indepedent trustee

Beneficiaries may include:
- Primary beneficiary
- Other immediate family members
- Future generations
- Charities

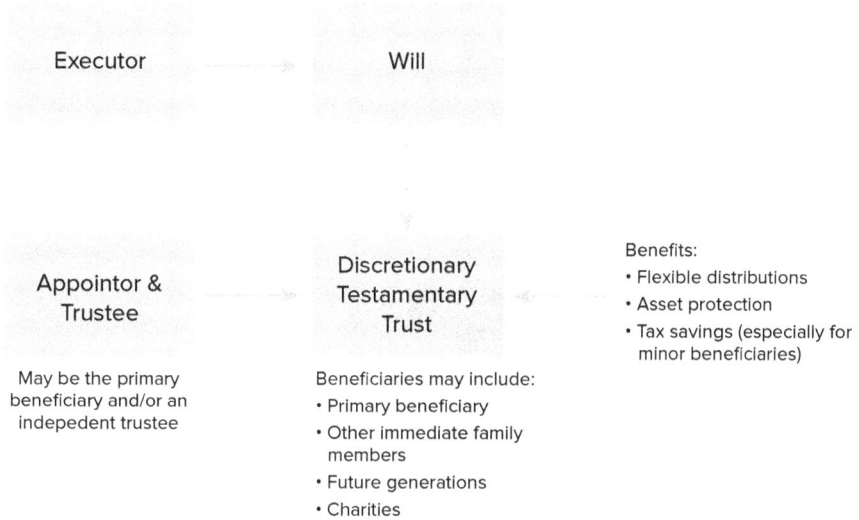

Figure 42: Testamentary trust structure

Protective testamentary trusts

Protective testamentary trusts are used when a family member is not in a position to take control of their inheritance in their own right due to physical or mental capacity. The trustee of a protective trust is responsible for ensuring the beneficiary receives the income needed to live comfortably, however unlike a standard testamentary trust, the beneficiary is prevented from gaining access to the capital of the trust.

A significant concern for parents with a disabled or wayward child is whether their child will be cared and provided for, beyond the parents' lifetime. Protective trusts are appropriate for families with a disabled child and can provide the peace of mind that long term protection can be provided for the child's inheritance.

Bloodline testamentary trusts

There's a saying in estate planning that you should never try to rule from the grave. In past generations, it was common for the family patriarch or matriarch to tie the estate up in knots so the only way beneficiaries could access the wealth left to them was by conforming to the rules and conventions set out in the will. Thankfully a lot has changed since then with most parents happy to see their families take control of the estate, leaving the inheritor to make their own decisions and forge their own path in life.

Having said that, family stewards are still concerned about ensuring an inheritance is not diluted by a family breakdown or other legal action. The family steward's preference is to see wealth passed for the benefit of their children and grandchildren, so giving thought in advance to the things that can go wrong is the first step in protecting your legacy.

Bloodline testamentary trusts are only unique in that they have special provisions to ensure that control of the trust cannot fall into the wrong hands. Broadly speaking, a bloodline trust is used to provide protection for beneficiaries in the event of death, family breakdown or mental incapacity. In any of these circumstances, the responsibility for looking after the trust will fall to a trustee nominated from within the family to look after the trust on behalf of the remaining beneficiaries. Where there is no one in the family able to fulfil the trustee role it is common to appoint one or more of the family's legal, financial or accounting advisers as an independent trustee.

With careful planning and consideration given to the future control of a testamentary trust, you can maximise the likelihood that the money you pass on will not fall into the wrong hands.

Case Study – Bloodline Testamentary Trust

Jane's elderly parents leave her a sizeable inheritance with the option of taking the money personally, or receiving it via a testamentary trust. Jane is married to Mike and they could do with the money as Mike's business has always struggled to reach its potential – the money would come in handy.

But based on the conversations Jane remembered having with her late father, she decides to receive the benefits in a testamentary trust, as she recalls him telling her that the inheritance was for her and her children. With the trust established, Jane is able to distribute trust income to herself, her three children and to Mike if she chooses.

Sometime later, Jane is diagnosed with terminal cancer and she is very concerned about the future of the trust as Mike's business is not in a great position. She fears that the trust funds will end up being used to pay off his business debts and then fund his lifestyle.

Fortunately, Jane's father had foreseen this possibility and had ensured that the testamentary trusts were bloodline trusts. This meant that if any of his children could no longer be the trustee of their trust due to their death, a marriage breakdown or mental incapacity, then the control of the trust at all times remains in the family bloodline. He had ensured that if Jane died, her husband could not take control of the trust.

When Jane passed away the terms of her late father's will required that Jane's sister and brother were appointed to the role of trustee to look after the trust for the benefit of Jane's children. The trust continued, with Jane's husband Mike receiving assistance with living expenses, school fees and family holidays, just as Jane and her father would have wanted it.

Superannuation

Where considerable wealth is tied up in superannuation, care must be taken to ensure the will is structured to deal with the passing of superannuation assets in the most tax effective manner possible. The trustee of your superannuation fund will usually determine who inherits your superannuation money in the event of your death and the form in which it is inherited. In making this determination, the trustee will take into account any death benefit nomination that you have made, the terms of your wills and the wishes of your beneficiaries.

Subject to the trust deed of your superannuation fund, the trustee can pay a death benefit in any or all of the following ways:

- As a lump sum to the surviving spouse or partner;

- As a pension to the surviving spouse or partner;

- As a lump sum to children;

- As a pension to children until they reach the age of 25; or,

- As a lump sum to the deceased person's estate. In this situation the amount will form part of the estate and may be inherited by a testamentary trust.

Other estate planning considerations

So far we have considered the decisions you will need to make in the event of death; however there are some important planning matters to ensure your affairs are satisfactorily attended to during your lifetime. By considering these matters carefully, you can ensure that the appropriate people take control of your affairs and any important conversations are held. These can be very sensitive periods for a family and the clear communication of your wishes enables everyone to understand your preferences in advance.

As a healthy adult, you may not foresee any circumstances where you would be incapable of making your own legal or financial decisions. However numerous situations can arise without warning - accidents, illness or loss of mental capacity - when you would be unable to safeguard your own interests.

The first of these is the appointment of a *guardian*. If you reach a stage during your lifetime when you are no longer able to deal with your own affairs, you will need a guardian to act on your behalf. The appointment of your guardian occurs under a legal document known as an *Enduring Power of Guardianship* (EPoG).

Your guardian will be able to make decisions on your behalf in respect of your living arrangements, care and medical treatments.

Next you will need to appoint an *attorney*. Similar to a guardian, your attorney is appointed to deal with financial matters. The appointment of your attorney occurs under a legal document known as an *Enduring Power of Attorney* (EPoA).

Your attorney 'stands in your shoes' when it comes to all financial decisions and is required to make the financial decisions you would have made, if you had the capacity to do so. Your attorney will be responsible to keep all your records, lodge your tax returns, and will have access to your bank accounts and all investments, so it is important to choose a person with knowledge of financial matters and someone who can be trusted implicitly by all family members.

If you are married, your partner is often the best person to appoint as your attorney and guardian; however, it always makes sense to have a substitute nominated in case your first nominee is not in a position to act. Family relationships are an important consideration when choosing a potential attorney and guardian, and care needs to be taken to avoid conflict and distrust amongst family members and any others who may have an interest in your well-being and your estate.

23. Giving Plan

"As you get older you will discover you have two hands, one for helping yourself, and one for helping others."

Audrey Hepburn

In our quest to live meaningful and purposeful lives, the act of giving to others creates a sense of fulfilment and satisfaction that cannot be experienced in many other ways. Over the years, I have observed that most of the successful people I have worked with have regarded giving as core to their sense of community and contribution. It is common when we are discussing values with a client that they will make *contribution to the community or giving back*, central to their family's values.

Giving appears in many forms other than donating money, and volunteering alone is estimated to contribute more than $25 billion each year to the Australian economy.[42] We should never overlook the benefits of volunteering particularly for those who have retired from the workforce. In Chapter 4, I discussed the PERMA formula for happiness, and the feelings of engagement, meaning and accomplishment are key sources of satisfaction for those who volunteer their skills and time for the causes they want to support.

Industrialist Andrew Carnegie was one of the wealthiest people who ever lived and he once wrote, "I will spend the first half of my life earning a fortune, and the second half of my life giving it away." Few of us will ever have the wealth to contribute the vast sums that the likes of Bill and Melinda Gates or Australia's Dick Smith or David Thomas have contributed over the years, however for those who have enjoyed considerable financial success, philanthropy is a growing priority.

The different motivations for giving are many and varied. To begin with there are considerable tax advantages available for donors as the federal government provides tax relief to encourage us to donate. The establishment of a charitable foundation is often timed to coincide with the sale of a major asset or family business. Proceeds from the asset sale that might otherwise be assessable income and therefore taxable, are strategically donated to a foundation to provide a long term legacy to fund the family's charitable interests. When established correctly, the contributions to the foundation are fully deductible.

Another benefit of giving is the opportunity to share the experience with family members. Family stewards will often describe the value of teaching their families the value of giving by creating a conversation around the family dinner table. Some families formalise the process by engaging younger generations in the investment strategy for the foundation and the selection of charitable recipients.

A personal connection to a charitable cause is another major reason for involvement. Where a family member has benefited from the services of a charity, family and friends are often deeply motivated to contribute, raise funds and donate skills and time to help others.

While there are many ways to contribute to society, sharing your wealth in a planned and considered way can be enormously rewarding and facilitate grassroots change that governments are unable to deliver. So how should you go about establishing a formal giving plan?

Keeping it simple

Direct giving represents the majority of charitable giving in Australia and is the primary source of funds for many Australian charities. Many of these direct donations are unplanned and are given in response to direct appeals to the public. Most people simply keep the receipts in order to claim the tax deduction.

With many Australians donating in an ad hoc way by giving small amounts to many charities, some believe that choosing one or two charities as your targets enables you to have greater impact with your giving.

Planned giving is the simplest way to formalise your charitable giving by allocating funds each year to gift directly to your chosen charities. While your donations may not be on the scale of a major philanthropist you can target your larger donations so that they make a difference to a cause you care deeply about.

This is a popular approach among families where there is a priority to teach their younger children the benefit of charitable giving. Matching the contribution of a child or grandchild to a charity also creates an opportunity to have a conversation with the child about the benefits of generosity.

For many families the conversation about the act of giving is an opportunity to pass on family values and create a culture of giving rather than taking.

Will bequests

Charitable gifts given in a will are known as specific bequests and many people use these gifts to leave money to their favourite charities. The gift of a bequest can provide a lasting legacy well beyond your lifetime and is an important source of funds for many charities.

With some extra thought in estate planning, a bequest to a charity could be made in a more tax-effective way, creating the potential for larger bequests.

For example, where a property or share portfolio is left as a gift to a charity, the assets may be subject to significant accrued capital gains. If the asset is given directly to a deductible gift recipient charity (DGR), then the assets may be transferred without tax being incurred by the charity. Alternately, if the gift were made instead as a lump sum of money the executor may need to sell down the shares first and incur the capital gains tax before the gift is made, and then the amount of money that can be distributed to the charity is smaller.

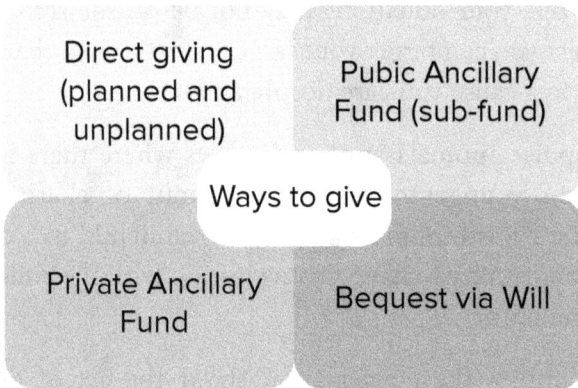

Direct giving (planned and unplanned)

Pubic Ancillary Fund (sub-fund)

Ways to give

Private Ancillary Fund

Bequest via Will

Figure 43: Key ways to give to charity

Charitable structures

For larger charitable gifts, a more formal structure may be appropriate. One of the advantages of using a charitable foundation, also known as a philanthropic trust, is that the gift may be given at one point in order to gain the tax benefit, while the decision to make charitable gift distributions may be deferred to a later period.

In making the decision to establish a charitable trust, families need to be aware that while they will maintain a level of control over where charitable gifts can be made in the future, no family member can ever benefit from the trust personally.

Many families use a charitable trust to engage the next generation of family members in the process of establishing and managing the trust. The management responsibilities extend to investing the assets of the trust and deciding where the charitable gifts are going to be directed each year.

The most common forms of charitable structures are Private Ancillary Funds (PAF) and Public Ancillary Funds (PuAF). Your choice will be driven by how much money you want to contribute to charitable causes and how much control you want over the process.

Philanthropy in Action

Cambodia is a country with gentle people and rich in history, with ancient temples and a deeply respectful culture. More recently, it is better known for the Pol Pot regime and the notorious Killing Fields. As a retired business owner, our client Jim had been helping a Cambodian charity on trips with various groups from Australia to help build homes for impoverished villagers.

On one such trip Jim saw the conditions in which children were being educated in a village and he concluded that for things to really change in Cambodia, it needed to begin by educating future generations. The current school, while serviceable, was too small to accommodate all age groups and the dirt floors turned to mud in the wet season. For education to be effective, the children needed a decent school to shelter from the blistering tropical heat and the rain.

Jim had the financial means, so he was able to 'guarantee' the funds needed to build the school so that planning and building could commence. He then set about encouraging others to contribute to the project.

Now, the school has been built and the children are sitting at their desks learning what six to ten year olds should be learning. The new structure will educate many generations into the future. While this is a simple case study, it showcases the real impact philanthropy can have on the lives of others.

Public ancillary funds

A public ancillary fund (PuAF) provides the easiest method of establishing a formal giving structure. Public funds are communal philanthropic structures that enable families to contribute to an existing fund by establishing a sub-fund. These contributions are often made to a named fund, reflecting the family's contribution to the larger fund. The donation to a PuAF is fully deductible and typically $50,000 or more is needed to establish a sub-fund.

The PuAF structure makes participation in philanthropy more accessible for smaller donors as the PuAF handles the administration, investment and governance activities, leaving the family to focus on deciding which charities they would like to support each year. This decision-making is done via an advisory committee enabling family members to have a say in the grant making decisions for the sub-fund.

Steps to establish a sub-fund in a Public ancillary fund (PuAF)

- Seek appropriate advice

- Choose a Public ancillary fund

- Decide how much you want to contribute

- Liaise with your tax adviser to ensure the structure is appropriate

- Establish your sub-fund

- Decide on your charitable causes.

Private ancillary funds

Private ancillary funds (PAF's) are also referred to as private or charitable foundations and they provide the greatest control for families wanting to create a significant long term legacy. The legal complexity involved with establishing and running a PAF means that it is best to have a minimum of $500,000 as the initial gift although larger amounts are needed to justify the long term PAF structure. [43]

A PAF will require its own trust deed and company trustee. The trustee company must have at least one independent director known as a responsible person, while the remaining directors may be family members. The trustee company is responsible for the administration and investment decisions of the PAF along with decisions made to give money to various charities in future years.

The decision to establish a PAF may coincide with a liquidity event like a business sale ensuring the tax deduction for the gift is available in the year of the asset sale, however the decision on how to give the money to charity can be spread over future years. A PAF must distribute a minimum of 5 percent of the opening value of the fund each year.

While the establishment and operation of a PAF may seem onerous compared with the public fund alternative, wealthy families should not discount the legacy value a PAF can create within a family. PAF's are ideal for families wanting to maintain control and establish a long term culture of giving within the family, particularly if the goal is to give across generations.

Steps to establishing a Private ancillary fund (PAF)

- Seek appropriate advice

- Liaise with your tax adviser to ensure the structure is appropriate

- Establish a special purpose Trustee Company

- Nominate the family members you want as Directors

- Nominate an independent Director who will be your Responsible Person

- Have a Trust Deed prepared

- Apply to the ATO and Australian Charities and Not-for profits Commission (ACNC) for charitable status

- Obtain an ABN

- Establish a bank account and make your initial donation

- Brief the directors of the trustee company of their duties and responsibilities

- Prepare an Investment Policy Statement

- Select and monitor the fund's investments

- Decide on a process to make charitable grants

- Oversee the ongoing administration, accounting and compliance for your PAF.

There is considerable responsibility associated with running a PAF and the right advisers will make this establishment process easy, so that you can focus on the benefits a charitable can bring to your family and the community.

24. Creating Family Harmony

"You don't choose your family. They are God's gift to you, as you are to them."

Desmond Tutu

None of us expects life to be perfect and I guess in the game of life some get luckier than others. However, preserving happy healthy relationships with the people we care most about is one of our most important indicators of long term happiness, so it's worth maximising your chances of success in this area.

In legacy planning, I see the potential to create the best of family relationships and yet there is also the potential for resentment and communication breakdown. In the first three sections of this book we have covered *purpose*, *strategic planning* and *investing*. By and large these areas impact you the most – get them right and you live comfortably, get them wrong and you are the one that suffers.

Legacy planning is different as it introduces the opinions and emotions of others into the equation, and deals with the big risks if something goes wrong, or potential resentment if the transfer of wealth from one generation to the next is not seen as fair. A young family without adequate insurance is courting dire financial consequences. An estate plan that is seen to favour one sibling, or the grant of a power of attorney to one son and not another can cause rifts between family members that are by and large avoidable and unnecessary.

Like most human interactions, the solution to creating family harmony lies in a commitment to open communication. This is why we have long advocated the need for parents, particularly family stewards, to get their adult children together to explain exactly how the legacy plan is structured and why. We call this the family meeting.

At the family meeting Mum and Dad, along with their adviser explain the family wealth structures and explain how the will is expected to be distributed. This is particularly important if siblings are to take joint control of a family trust structure and will be required to work together in the long term to manage the assets. If an independent executor and trustee is to be appointed to manage the estate, this is the time to explain why so that when the will is being administered everyone is clear on the parent's wishes.

The family meeting begins with the parents outlining their values and their hopes for the legacy to be passed from one generation to the next, then there's an explanation of the family's trust and company structures, and finally an explanation of the wills. The opportunity for adult children to ask questions, clarify and understand the issues is a positive first step towards a successful outcome.

The idea of a 'no surprises' policy is often the best way to promote long term harmony in any family and while there are no guarantees, clarity and understanding can often go a long way towards avoiding conflict.

HONEST CONVERSATIONS → MANAGE TRADE-OFFS → ESTABLISH DIRECTION

ON GOING COURSE CORRECTIONS

Section Take-outs

....

....

....

....

....

....

....

....

....

....

PART V

WORKING WITH A
FINANCIAL PROFESSIONAL

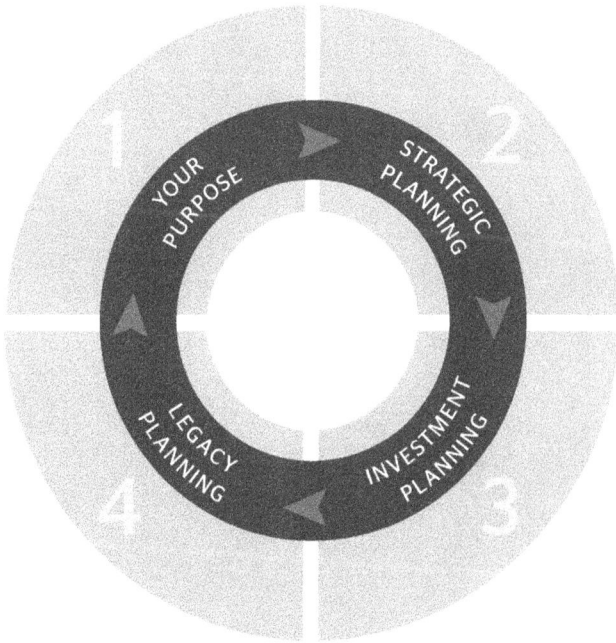

25. Working with a Financial Professional

"Being rich is having money, being wealthy is having time."

Henry Ward Beecher

By reputation alone, it is understandable why many Australians are reluctant to engage with a financial planner or wealth manager. Almost daily, news headlines tell the sorry tale of financial scandals and investor losses. The situation is not surprising, because under current laws in Australia, a one-week financial planning course is enough to enable you to become a licensed financial adviser. Yet it takes many years of study and personal experience to become an effective adviser in almost any field. Little wonder consumers are wary.

At the core of the problem is the structure of the industry itself. Traditionally, the financial services industry has been *sales-centric* rather than *advice-centric* and the difference between these two models will determine the experience you have with your adviser.

Sales-centric model

The traditional or sales-centric model of financial services begins with a profit motive and the need for product sales. In this model, institutions produce their products with the best possible profit margins, and then look to ways to distribute and sell their product to as many customers as possible.

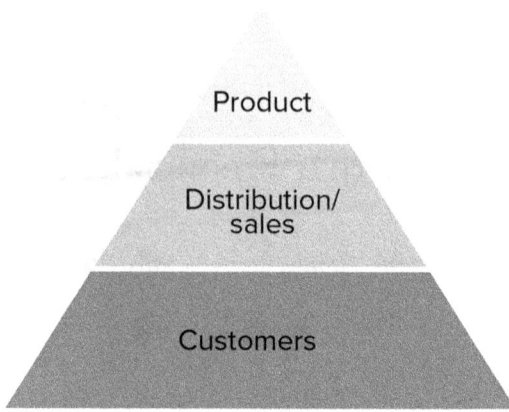

Figure 44: Sales-centric model of financial services.

In the 1960s and 1970s, when our financial needs were less complex, this model worked well for most consumers who purchased insurance policies and investments from company salesmen, and bought and sold shares with stockbrokers.

Just as complexity has increased, so have consumer expectations as they have become more reliant on real financial advice. There is greater awareness of the need for tax planning, proper diversification and long-term planning. In the sales-centric model there is a clear conflict between the what the consumer needs - *advice*, and what the salesperson wants which is a *product sale*.

This results in a transaction that has just enough advice included to meet the minimum compliance requirements to get the product sale. There is little motivation for the adviser to provide advice in a truly comprehensive way, because the time spent helping you would prevent them moving onto the next customer and the next sale.

Then once the sale is complete, there is little commitment to ongoing service because it takes time and does not always result in further sales. The traditional model tends to be seen in the larger banks, stockbroking firms and other financial institutions where the adviser's interests are clearly aligned with their employer's, rather than their clients'.

Ultimately, this structure forces the good advisers to leave because they feel conflicted and they are unable to provide the advice they know they should be providing. It also tends to leave the slick sales people working successfully in these institutions with bigger targets to sell more product.

For some institutions in Australia, there is a clear incentive for their advisers to sell in-house products over other potentially cheaper or better products, as the institution's vertically integrated model rewards those who maximise the organisation's profits.

Client-centric model

The client-centric approach turns the traditional model upside down as it begins with the client's best interests as the first consideration. Bottom line, it begins with you. Your needs, your goals and priorities, your concerns. As you have read through this book you will have noticed the emphasis on understanding all of your information in the right context, *before* you start making financial decisions.

A client-centric adviser won't rush you to make a decision and will patiently listen and gather information so they know what's important to you before they start providing advice. Just the use of the word client instead of customer suggests a different, more caring approach.

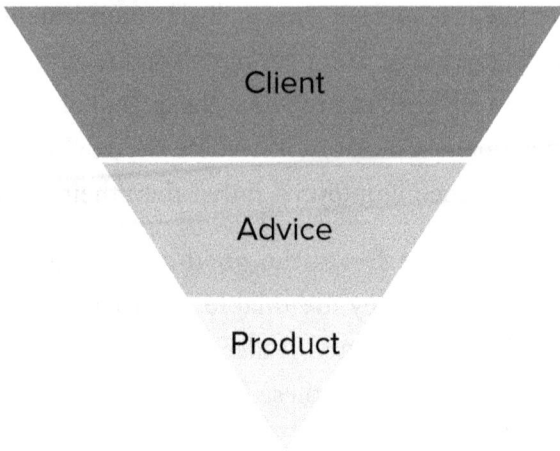

Figure 45: Client-centric model of financial services

Rather than a focus on getting sales, a client-centric adviser will be focused on helping you achieve your goals. There will likely be an expectation of a long term relationship where your progress is reviewed, discipline is maintained and where changes to your strategy are made when necessary.

Great financial advisers are like an orchestra conductor. They surround themselves with a network of other professionals who work together to identify and resolve issues as they arise. Rather than it being the adviser's first priority, selection of the financial products you need will be last step in the client-centric advice process.

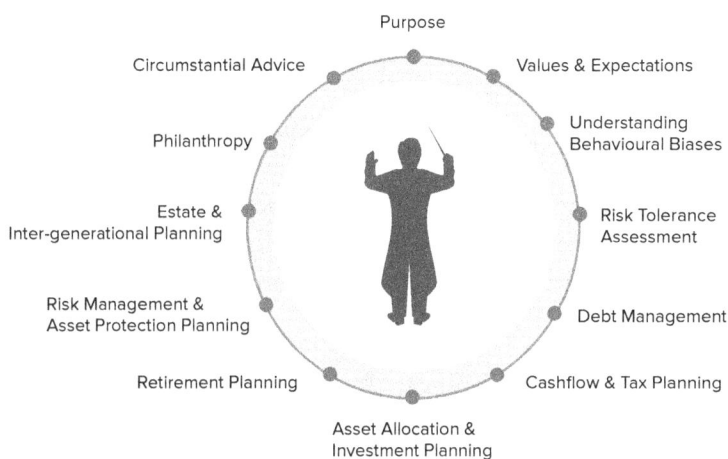

Figure 46: Wealth manager as orchestra conductor

Should you work with a financial professional?

Your first decision will be whether you want to engage with a professional at all. Your decision will be driven by many factors such as the complexity of your affairs, your knowledge, how much time you have, how organised you are, and how badly you think you need help.

Your own personality will provide some clues around how well you will work with an adviser and the type of adviser you would be most suited to working with.

Some people love the detail around financial matters and take pleasure in trying to work things out for themselves. They read the financial press widely and see little value in paying for financial advice. These people are *Self-directed*. As the name suggests, the self-directed are less likely to seek out financial planning advice because they believe

233

they have the skill and aptitude to do the job themselves and they prefer to spend their own time researching the information they need, rather than paying someone else to do the work. They may spend many hours working out their own plan, calculating taxes and managing their portfolio. The self-directed like to be in control and will seek information from many sources including friends, colleagues and online to patch together all the information needed to form a strategy. Self-directed people are the least likely to value the services of a professional financial adviser, but may rely on their accountant or stockbroker for ideas.

The next group are the *Validators*. As the name suggests, validators may consider themselves to be on top of their financial affairs but value the security of a second opinion. They will often seek out advice on specific pieces of their financial puzzle but may not see the value in engaging in comprehensive advice. Validators are generally savvy on financial matters and often enjoy the challenge of working things out for themselves. Where they do seek out professional advice, it will be to validate their own ideas and conclusions. Validators are often a little frustrated by financial advisers. This is because validators prefer to choose only the services *they* want, while the professional adviser often feels obliged to do things comprehensively. This normally results in the validator shopping around until they find an adviser who will do business for them on their terms.

Finally, we have the *Delegators*. Delegators understand that there is more to life than money. They are very happy to outsource certain things in their lives to others, in order to free up their own time to focus on the things that are important to them. Delegators are often very successful in their own fields, and their success is often *because* they understand that effective delegation enables them to be even more successful in their own endeavours. They will rarely do something themselves when they know someone else can do it better.

Other delegators simply accept that they don't have the knowledge they need to look after their own financial affairs and will seek out a relationship with someone they trust.

When it comes to the design and implementation of a comprehensive financial plan, delegators prefer to work with a professional. They will be very engaged in the conversation around what success looks like to them and what needs to happen, they just won't want to do all the work themselves.

Delegators often have greater wealth and complexity but limited time, so the idea of paying for comprehensive advice makes more sense to them. Most importantly, they recognise two critical factors in living life successfully. First, they accept that they do not need to know everything about everything to be successful, and second, they have an ability to build relationships with people they know will be able to help them.

As you read about the three different kinds of investor; the *self-directed*, the *validator* and *delegator*, one of the three descriptions will have resonated more for you than the others. The question most people should ask is, *"which of these three approaches will best suit me, and lead me to the financial success I want?"*

For many self-directed investors, trying to work with a professional adviser will be a waste of time. They are far more likely to research online, subscribe to investment newsletters, and rely on a network of like-minded friends and colleagues.

Similarly, validators will tend to start out by doing their own research and will use similar sources to self-directed investors, but may look for professional advice in certain areas. They will normally use an accountant, a stockbroker or an adviser who is happy to charge by the hour and provide advice on a limited scope basis.

In recent times *robo-advice*, or online investing is becoming more available in Australia. These online services provide low cost portfolio services, and the development of this sector will unfold in the same way online stockbroking evolved in the 1990s. Self-directed and validator investors will find robo-advice very attractive for its ease of use and low cost.

The final group, the delegators, will choose to work with a financial professional and it is then a matter of how best to choose one.

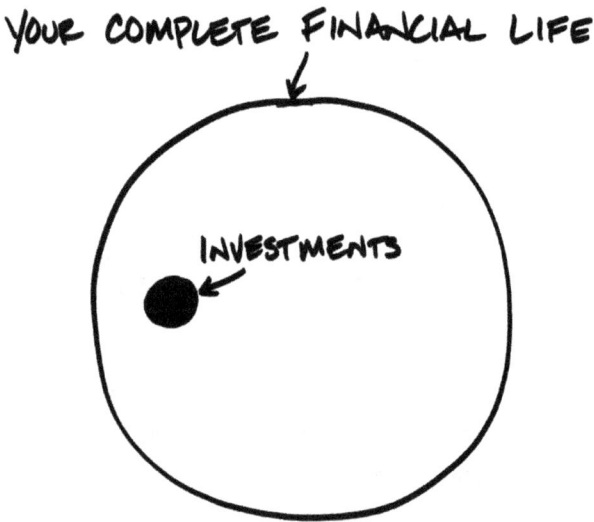

YOUR COMPLETE FINANCIAL LIFE

INVESTMENTS

26. Finding the Right Adviser

"Quality is never an accident. It is always the result of intelligent effort."

John Ruskin

Having decided to engage an adviser, you will be looking for a trusted adviser and not a salesperson. Ideally you will also find someone who will help you get your whole financial life in order, not just sort out a product transaction. A strong referral from a friend or colleague is normally a good starting point although you will need to do a little research and ask a few questions to ensure you choose wisely.

Firstly, you will want to find someone who is used to working with people who are similar to you. For example, there are advisers with specific expertise in areas like working with business owners, medical specialists, or law firm partners and barristers. Some advisers specialise in small clients and social security issues, while others specialise in helping wealthier clients with greater complexity. Having an adviser who is familiar with the issues you may be facing will be a great head start.

When you meet an adviser for the first time, you will probably expect the conversation to be all about money. Having read this book, you will be well prepared for how the financial planning process works, what's involved, and the conversations you should be having.

As you are speaking to potential advisers, you will be forming an opinion of them: good, bad or indifferent. You should also be aware that the best advisers will also be forming an opinion about you. In my experience, the best advisers will not accept every new client who walks through their door; in fact, they are very discerning about whom they accept as a new client. From the adviser's perspective, their greatest asset is their reputation, so by only accepting those clients they want to work with, they will be more certain they can really add significant value. This active client selection process results in good outcomes for both the adviser and the client.

You will generally get the feeling when you are in the presence of a real professional. If you feel you are being sold to, then move on. However, if the process is clear, logical and transparent, you will probably feel you are on the right track.

Does the adviser have a formal advice process?

If you are going to engage an adviser, you will want to know that everything that's promised is being delivered. The more complex your affairs, the more certainty you will want that everything is being dealt with in a timely manner. Good advisers will be able to demonstrate that their systems and processes are adequate to meet your needs.

All good financial advisers have a formalised advice process like the one shown in Figure 47, and it is important that they do. Because wealth management can be so complex, the benefit of a process is that nothing falls down the cracks and gets forgotten or missed. The biggest benefit of a formal advice process is that you know where it is going, and what you can expect at each step of the way. The process also enables the adviser to be very thorough in their work, and enables their support team to know what needs to be done every step of the way.

Many financial advisers offer the world upfront but deliver very little when it comes to the crunch, so working with an adviser who can demonstrate a long track record of delivering quality advice backed by all the systems they need, will be an important consideration.

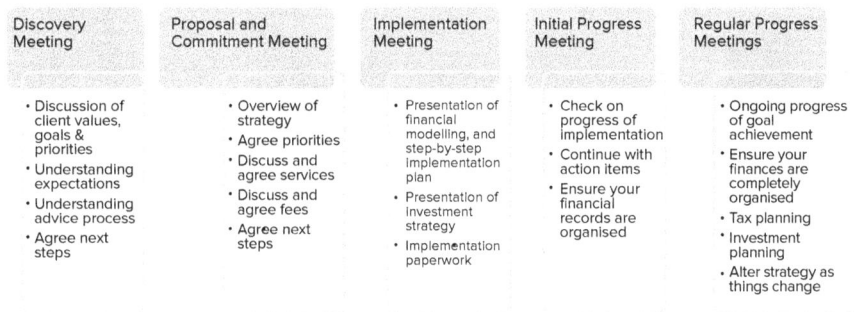

Discovery Meeting	Proposal and Commitment Meeting	Implementation Meeting	Initial Progress Meeting	Regular Progress Meetings
• Discussion of client values, goals & priorities • Understanding expectations • Understanding advice process • Agree next steps	• Overview of strategy • Agree priorities • Discuss and agree services • Discuss and agree fees • Agree next steps	• Presentation of financial modelling, and step-by-step implementation plan • Presentation of investment strategy • Implementation paperwork	• Check on progress of implementation • Continue with action items • Ensure your financial records are organised	• Ongoing progress of goal achievement • Ensure your finances are completely organised • Tax planning • Investment planning • Alter strategy as things change

Figure 47: Comprehensive wealth management process

It may also be worth asking how many clients your adviser looks after. Many advisers have hundreds of clients who are no more than names on a list. The best advisers will look after a relatively small number of clients and provide a high quality, proactive planning service.

Qualifications

When it only takes one week of study to attain the minimum requirement to be a financial planner it will pay to ensure the person you are dealing with has the skills and experience to fulfil for your particular needs.

One way to identify a quality adviser is to assess their qualifications. Finding one with formal business or finance qualifications is a good start. The highest education standard for financial advisers around the world is the Certified Financial Planner® designation, a standard that requires considerable time and commitment to attain.[44]

Professional Designations	Academic Qualifications
Certified Financial Planner (CFP)	Master of Financial Planning
Accredited Investment Fiduciary (AIF)	Bachelor of Commerce
Chartered Accountant (CA)	Graduate Diploma Financial Planning
Certified Practicing Accountant (CPA)	Graduate Diploma Applied Finance and Investment
Chartered Financial Analyst (CFA)	Advanced Diploma Financial Planning
SMSF Specialist Advisor (SSA)	

Figure 48: Professional qualifications and designations

Just because an adviser holds a degree or designation does not guarantee that they will provide you with a quality advice service, although it will be an indication that your adviser has made the investment in themselves to complete university qualifications and meet higher industry standards.

Consistent investment philosophy

Your chosen adviser should have a consistent, clearly documented investment philosophy that does not confuse investing with speculation. I have seen many adviser businesses over the years where there is little or no consistency from one client portfolio to the next. This is an indication that they fly by the seat of their pants and create portfolios based on their latest great ideas. The biggest problem with this approach is that because their client portfolios are all so different, some clients do really well, while others languish. This leaves your chances of success to be something of a raffle which may be fine for the adviser's own money, but it certainly isn't an acceptable way to manage money for clients.

There are many different approaches to money management and the evidence based approach set out earlier in Part III is just one example of an investment philosophy that can be consistently implemented for clients over time.

There is a growing movement around the world for leading financial adviser firms to become accredited as *Fiduciaries*. The Latin word *Fiducia* simply means trust. Investment fiduciary firms submit their investment process to an annual audit process, where their decision making process is accredited against a global quality standard which is analogous to the ISO 9000 standard for continuous improvement. These standards are set by the Centre for Fiduciary Excellence CEFEX.[45] This is one additional way that potential clients can take comfort from an adviser firm.

Independence

Australian investors are clearly confused when it comes to choosing an 'independent' financial adviser. A recent study, found that 14 per cent of customers visiting a Commonwealth Bank branded financial planner thought they were getting independent financial advice.[46] The confusion is even greater when the adviser firm is branded differently to the umbrella institution. The same survey found that 55 per cent of consumers visiting Commonwealth Bank owned Financial Wisdom, thought they were getting independent advice too.

So what does independent mean? In reality independent means that there is no relationship between the advisory firm and a product manufacturer. A conflict would arise if an adviser in recommending an organisation's product received a benefit for doing so.

Today many organisations are 'vertically integrated', which means the financial product and the advice are sourced from under the same roof. While there is a potential for conflict here, many good advisers work under vertically integrated models and can explain how their services work in relation to their parent company. Others have no choice but to recommend in-house products. If you are unsure about your options, ask whether the adviser can recommend products other than those offered by the parent company. If you want to check where the ultimate control behind your adviser lies, you can check on the *Financial Adviser Register* at www.moneysmart.gov.au, this will guide you on the questions you may need to ask.

In Australia there are few truly independent advisers even though many will make the claim. Ultimately you need to ask the right questions before you receive the advice to protect your interests.

How will your adviser be paid?

Until the federal government changed the law in 2013, the vast majority of advisers earned commissions for the placement of investment funds. Today almost all advisers in Australia charge fees for the services they provide. As you review different advice services you will find both the price and the quality of advice will vary considerably.

Regardless of how your adviser collects fees, the most important issue is transparency. You are completely entitled to have a *full and clear* understanding of all fees you pay so that you are in a position to make an assessment of the value you are receiving. You should be in a position to do this before you start a relationship with the adviser and on an ongoing basis.

Strategic advice

Most advisers will charge fees for the preparation and implementation of a financial plan and for continuing strategic advice. These fees will be for the initial strategic plan and any costs associated with maintaining your strategy on an ongoing basis. The more complex your affairs, the more work your adviser will need to do in the areas of tax and other planning so you will need to factor this in when considering the fee you are willing to pay.

These fees can be charged in a few different ways and may be presented in any combination of those below:

- Hourly rate for services performed.

- Agreed fee for work completed.

- Monthly retainer for services provided.

Investment management

Many advisers will charge a discrete fee for the management of money and this fee can be charged as a percentage of the funds invested, or as an agreed fixed fee. For larger portfolio clients, it is common for advisers to charge a percentage of assets invested, but to include a wide range of planning and review services in addition to investment management.

When considering any proposal for services, you must be sure that you are comfortable with both the fee, and the scope of the services being provided. If the proposed services only relate to portfolio management, you may need to consider your need for a more comprehensive approach. It is very rare that an investor will be well served just on the basis of having their money managed, without proper regard for tax and other strategic issues.

Life insurance and home loan products

It is still customary for advisers to be remunerated by way of product commissions for life insurance and home loan products. Once again you are entitled to know exactly what the adviser will receive for the placement of an insurance policy or home loan.

As a final word on fees, you will generally get what you pay for as comprehensive, high quality advice requires time and careful consideration before it is presented. You will just need to ensure that your adviser is prepared to provide you with a clear and concise estimate of fees along with a description of the services provided, before you authorise them to commence work.

Many advisers will provide all of these services and so the fee you pay may end up being a combination of each of the fees I have outlined above. The manner of fee calculation and collection does not matter greatly as long as you have complete transparency over the amount being charged and you are comfortable that you are receiving value.

Financial Adviser Due Diligence Checklist

1. Is the financial adviser primarily interested in me and my family, or my money?

2. Is the adviser a good listener?

3. Does the adviser work with other people with needs like mine?

4. Is the service offer comprehensive or a transactional service?

5. Can the adviser articulate a clear value proposition?

6. Can the adviser articulate a clear investment philosophy?

7. What is the adviser's process for ensuring they are on top of my affairs?

8. Is the adviser a one-man band, or part of a larger team?

9. Is the adviser independent or aligned to an institution?

10. Are fees, charges and services provided clearly documented in advance?

11. Are the adviser's qualifications and experience appropriate?

12. Does the adviser speak in clear language or in 'financial speak'?

13. Is the adviser supportive and collaborative, or condescending?

14. How often will we meet?

15. What can I do if I'm not happy?

What can you expect?

The decision to appoint a financial professional to help you manage your financial affairs should not deliver a marginal benefit. If you have chosen the right firm and the right adviser, the benefits to you should be considerable. Ideally you will have a feeling of being incredibly well organised with everything up to date and important future tasks identified and scheduled for completion.

Your *Purpose* will have been clearly defined with a written statement of your values and goals, and you will be clear on your priorities. Your *Strategic Plan* will identify the best possible way to combine your spending and saving to give you the best shot at your ideal life. Your *Investment Plan* will be carefully considered and implemented to maximise the probability of success in an uncertain environment. And finally, your *Legacy Plan* will ensure your estate, your insurances and your charitable interests are in perfect order.

Having travelled to meet financial advisers all over Australia and the world, I have identified five characteristics that I always see in the best advisers:

Advocate – as your advocate they will always put your interests ahead of their own. They will always tell you the truth about your situation and provide the best options for you to consider. They can navigate their way through ethical issues and conflicts to ensure your best interests are always considered first.

Expert – now more than ever expertise is required to build the right strategy taking account of all the complexities we are faced with. Part of a great adviser's expertise is to identify issues, and to know when a matter is beyond their scope. This is when their network of like-minded professionals is engaged to help solve your issue.

Objective Voice – in a world full of choices and uncertainty, it is easy to get caught up in the emotion of what is going on around us. This is particularly the case during periods of great uncertainty in our own lives, or when there is great uncertainty in the world around us. A good adviser will listen to your concerns and tease out the issues driving those feelings in order to provide practical long-term answers.

Coach – no one succeeds alone and despite the best strategy, doubts and fears inevitably arise. Great advisers hold people accountable to the things they have said they'd do, and offer encouragement to help stay the course. And if things do get off track, there's a gentle nudge from the coach back in the direction of success.

Guardian – Beyond these experiences, there is a long term role for the adviser as a kind of lighthouse keeper, scanning the horizon for issues that may affect your situation and identifying risks before they arise. This helps you remain focused on the things that matter most in your life other than money.

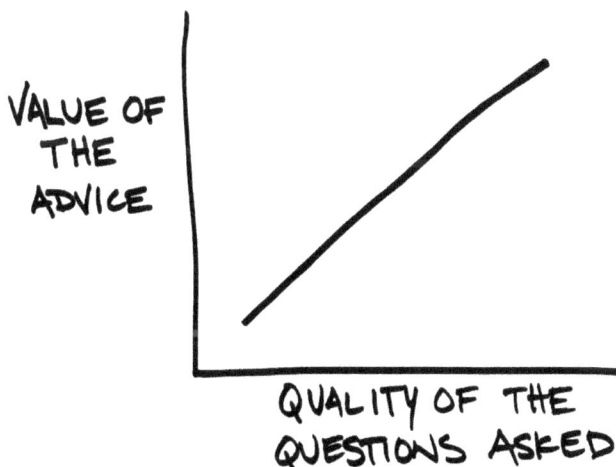

VALUE OF THE ADVICE

QUALITY OF THE QUESTIONS ASKED

Section Take-outs

....

....

....

....

....

....

....

....

....

....

27. So What Next?

"The best way to get started is to quit talking and start doing."

Walt Disney

I wanted to write this book to help people and I hope the investment you have made in reading it has been worthwhile. When I am asked why I enjoy working as a financial adviser the answer is easy. I get to help people, make an honest living, and have the time I need outside work to enjoy a great life.

My goal was to provide you with a common sense guide to wealth, investing and an inspiring life – I hope I have done that.

I hope that you can use the wealth management process I have outlined to help you take control of your finances and to be clearer about what really matters in your life. Whether you choose to engage with a financial adviser or do it yourself, having a plan will significantly increase your chances of success.

From time to time it will be important to check in and make sure you are living a life without regrets. Are your close relationships where they need to be? Are you finding the right balance between living today and being secure tomorrow? Let's say you had all the money you need to be financially successful and free, would you still be doing what you're doing? Are you making time for your goals, dreams and passions?

There's little point in being so busy living life that we forget to enjoy those simple things that give us the most pleasure. Remember that effective delegation saves you time and ultimately money and there's little to be gained from being a busy fool. If you can outsource things in your life to experts, you free up time to do more of what you are really good at, and you create time for more of the things you enjoy.

Over twenty years I have had the privilege of working side by side with wonderful families who have become wealthy *slowly*. They have done everything laid out in this book, from being clear on their values, documenting their goals, working to a strategy, investing wisely, designing their legacy and then, they have remained committed and disciplined through periods of personal and external uncertainty.

Great outcomes require commitment. As you embark on your wealth management journey, remember that *real wealth* is defined by the richness of your life and the lives of those you care about. By focusing on enjoying great experiences with the people you love, rather than things, you will be well on the way to living an *inspiring life*.

Enjoy the journey.

Table of Figures

Table of Figures

References

Chapter 1

[1] Source: ABS Australian Historical Population Statistics 2008 (Cat. No. 3105.0.65.001); ABS Deaths, Australia, 2009.

Chapter 4

[2] Sinek, S., Start with Why, How Great Leaders Inspire Everyone to take Action, Penguin, 2009.

[3] Kasser, T., The High Price of Materialism, MIT Press, 2002.

Chapter 6

[4] Mandela, N., Long Walk to Freedom, Abacus, 1994.

[5] www.inc.com.

Chapter 7

[6] Australia Today – Part 1, A look at lifestyle, financial security and retirement in Australia. www.mlc.com.au/australiatoday.

[7] Australia Today – Part 2, A look at lifestyle, financial security and retirement in Australia. www.mlc.com.au/australiatoday.

Chapter 10

[8] Drew, M, and Walk, A, (2014), How Safe are Safe Withdrawal Rates in Retirement? An Australian Perspective, (Financial Services Institute of Australasia), Sydney.

Chapter 12

[9] The Economist, Rich Man's Burden, 14th June 2001.

[10] King, C. F., Confident Future: Creating a Sound Financial Future for Women after Divorce, White Paper, Capital Partners Private Wealth, 2016.

[11] Ibid.

[12] Ibid.

Chapter 14

[13] Dimson E, Marsh P, Staunton M, The Triumph of the Optimists: 101 Years of Global Investment Returns. Princeton University Press, 2002.

[14] Source MLC.

[15] Source for 1913 and 1963: Historical Statistics of the United States: Colonial Times to 1970/U.S. Dept. of Commerce. Source for 2013: United States Department of Labor, Bureau of Labor Statistics, Economic Statistics, Consumer Price Index – Average Price Data.

[16] Center for Research on Securities Prices. CRSP 1-10 (Market) January 1926 – December 2015.

[17] In Australian dollars. Global electronic order book (largest 50 exchanges). Source: World Federation of Exchanges.

[18] Fama E, and French, K, Luck Versus Skill in the Cross Section of Mutual Fund Returns, Journal of Finance.

[19] SPIVA Australia Scorecard– Standard and Poor's Index versus Active, S&P Dow Jones Indices, Mid-Year 2015.

Chapter 15

[20] Fama, E, and French, K., Cross Section of Expected Stock Returns, Journal of Finance, No. 47 (1992).

[21] Australian market vs. Bank Bills: Market is S&P/ASX 300 (Accumulation) Index. Bank bills is Bloomberg AusBond Bank Bill Index. Jan 1980 to Dec 2015. There are 241 overlapping 15-year periods, 301 overlapping 10-year periods, 361 overlapping 5-year periods and 409 overlapping 1-year periods.

[22] Australian Stock Exchange.

[23] Banz, Rolf. W. 1981. "The Relationship between Return and Market Value of Common Stocks." Journal of Financial Economics 9 (1): 3–18.

[24] Center for Research in Securities Prices, The University of Chicago.

[25] Small is Dimensional Australia Small Cap Index. Large is MSCI Australia Index. Jan 1974 to Dec 2015. There are 313 overlapping 15-year periods, 373 overlapping 10-year periods, 433 overlapping 5-year periods and 481 overlapping 1-year periods.

[26] Source: Yahoo Finance.

[27] Source: Returns Program, S&P Australia BMI Value Index and S&P Australia Growth Index.

[28] Australian Value vs Growth. Value is Fama/French Australian Value Index. Growth is Fama/French Australian Growth Index. There are 301 overlapping 15-year periods; 361 overlapping 10-year periods; 421 overlapping 5-year periods, and 385 overlapping 1-year periods.

[29] Novy-Marx R, The Other Side of Value: The Gross Profitability Premium, Journal of Financial Economics, Volume 108, April 2013.

[30] High is Dimensional Australia High Profitability Index. Low is Dimensional Low Profitability Index. There are 217 overlapping 15-year periods, 277 overlapping 10-year periods, 337 overlapping 5-year periods, and 385 overlapping 1-year periods.

Chapter 16

[31] Ibbotson, R.G. and Kaplan, P.D., Does Asset Allocation Policy Explain 40, 90 or 100 Percent of Performance, Financial Analysts Journal, January 2000.

[32] Brinson G.P, Singer, B.D., Beebower, G.L., Determinants of Portfolio Performance II: An Update, Financial Analysts Journal, May 1991.

[33] Cash is the Bloomberg AusBond Bank Bill Index and Shares is the S&P/ASX All Ordinaries Index. January 1980 to December 2015. Annual Rebalancing. Source: Morningstar. Analysis: Capital Partners Consulting.

[34] Markowitz, H.M. (March 1952). "Portfolio Selection". The Journal of Finance 7 (1): 77–91.

[35] Data is the annual return to 31 December, 2015. Data used for each asset class is as follows: Australian Large: S&P/ASX100 Index, Australian Small: S&P/ASX Small Ordinaries Index, Australian Value: S&P Australia BMI Value Index (gross div. AUD), Global Large: MSCI World Index, (net div. AUD) Global Small: MSCI World Small Cap Index (net div. AUD), Global Value: MSCI World

Value Index (net div., AUD), Emerging Markets: MSCI Emerging Markets Index (net div. AUD), Property: S&P Global REIT Index (net div.), Cash: Bloomberg AusBond Bank Bill Index, Fixed Interest: Barclays Global Aggregate Bond Index (hedged to AUD). S&P/ASX data reproduced with the permission of S&P Index Services Australia. MSCI data copyright MSCI 2015, all rights reserved. Securities and commodities data provided by Bloomberg. Barclays indices copyright Barclays 2015. The S&P data are provided by Standard & Poor's Index Services Group.

Indices are not available for direct investment. Their performance does not reflect the expenses associated with the management of an actual portfolio.

Chapter 17

[36] Source: Returns 2.0 and Morningstar Direct. Analysis: Capital Partners Consulting. Portfolios are rebalanced monthly and all income is reinvested. Highest and lowest returns are calculated from rolling one-month periods. Australian large is DFA Australian large index. Australian Value is Fama/French Australian Value index. Australian Small is DFA Australian Small company index. Global large is DFA Global large ex-Australia Index. Global Value is Fama/French Global ex-Australia Value index. Global Small is DFA Global ex-Australia Small Company Index. Emerging markets is DFA Emerging Markets Value Index. Property is S&P/ASX 300 A-REIT Index. Fixed Interest is Bloomberg AusBond Bank Bill Index.

Chapter 18

[37] Dalbar Inc. "Quantitative Analysis of Investment Behavior", 2015.

[38] Daily Standard & Poor's index data is provided by SPICE. The monthly UBS data provided by Bloomberg. S&P/ASX data reproduced with the permission of S&P Index Services Australia. UBS data reproduced with the permission of UBS Australia Ltd. Indices are not available for direct investment. Their performance does not reflect the expenses associated with the management of an actual portfolio.

[39] Kahneman, D. & Tversky, A., Prospect Theory: An Analysis of Decision under Risk, Econometrica, 47(2), pp. 263-291, March 1979.

Chapter 19

[40] Juru, Sheunesu G. and Johnson, J., A Case for Index Fund Investing in Australia. Vanguard Research, July 2015.

[41] Source: Morningstar Direct. Analysis: Capital Partners Consulting.

Chapter 23

[42] Volunteering Australia, Australian Bureau of Statistics.

[43] Australian Philanthropic Services.

Chapter 26

[44] CFP® and Certified Financial Planner are certification marks owned by the Financial Planning Standards Board and are licensed for use by the Financial Planning Association of Australia.

[45] www.cefex.org

[46] Roy Morgan Research, Confusion with Financial Planner Independence Continues, Article 5746, August 2014.

"David has a deep understanding of finance, but his insight and years of experience are highlighted when the behavioural aspects of finance are explained in the context of a higher purpose for every reader. Every investor should invest their time to read this book!"

Alex Potts
President and CEO, Loring Ward Group
Author of *The Wealth Solution*

"There's so much information available today about investing, it's hard to know where to start. But if there's one book that Australian investors should read, it's this one. David's starting-point is the end investor, what's important to them and what they're looking to achieve. His investment philosophy is based not on his opinion but on independent, peer-reviewed and time-tested evidence about how best to invest. In 20 years' time most Australians will invest this way."

Robin Powell
Editor, *The Evidence-based Investor*

"The investment industry's penchant for jargon, the ongoing blurring of the line between selling and advising (and the odd financial scandal for good measure), have created an environment where trust has been eroded. The time has come for 'less words, more action' to place clients at the heart of everything we do. I commend David Andrew's new book 'Wealth with Purpose' to anyone seeking to learn more about starting the financial planning process with the destination in mind - an alignment of values, goals, planning and, most importantly, improved outcomes."

Dr Michael E. Drew
Professor of Finance, Griffith University
Director, Drew, Walk & Co.

"This book provides genuine and reliable insights, that if followed, will see you make great decisions with money for the rest of your life. If your goal is to live a happy and fulfilling life, making smart money decisions and investing wisely, you should find the time to read this book."

Peter Mancell
Chairman, Global Association of Independent Advisors
Geneva, Switzerland

261

About the Author

David Andrew is founder and CEO of Capital Partners Private Wealth, the largest independently owned and non-aligned advisory firm in Perth, Western Australia. His belief that real wealth management fundamentally and positively changes people's lives, lies behind the comprehensive approach Capital Partners takes in advising clients.

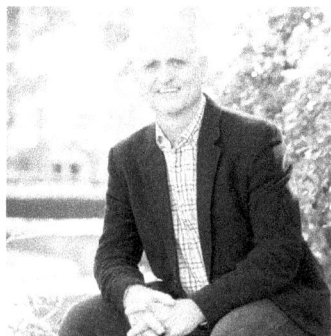

He believes that we are all presented with opportunities that enable us to significantly improve the quality of our lives, and the way we approach our relationship with money is one of these opportunities. By starting with your purpose - your values, goals and priorities - he believes you can lay the foundations for a happier more fulfilled life.

He has guided Capital Partners to a number of firsts which include:

- achieving the globally recognised fiduciary standard CEFEX, the highest standard of investment governance an advisory firm can attain;
- founding membership of GAIA, the Global Association of Independent Advisors; and,
- establishing Smartinvestor.tv, an online video resource to help investors better understand investing.

David lives in Perth with his wife Robyn and three sons.